UWENZI

UWENZi

The Pan-African Factor, A 21st-Century View

David O. Akombo

Baruti I. Katembo

Kmt G. Shockley

authorHOUSE®

AuthorHouse™
1663 Liberty Drive
Bloomington, IN 47403
www.authorhouse.com
Phone: 1 (800) 839-8640

Published by AuthorHouse   07/13/2016

ISBN: 978-1-5049-6283-4 (sc)
ISBN: 978-1-5049-6284-1 (e)

Library of Congress Control Number: 2015919046

Cover Concept and Design: Baruti I. Katembo
Giraffes Around Watering Hole Photo (on cover): Martin Harvey (photographer),
www.wildimagesonline.com
African Diaspora Global Distribution Map Image (on cover): University of
Notre Dame Department of Africana Studies, www.africana.nd.edu
Kuba Cloth Photo (on cover): Africa Imports, www.africaimports.com
Major editing and associated consultation: Nowick Gray (owner – HyperLife Editing Services),
www.hyperlife-editing.com

Akombo, David O., Katembo, Baruti I., and Shockley, Kmt G.
UWENZI: *The Pan-African Factor, A 21st-Century View*
Summary: Provides 21st-century dialogue on selected strategies (and impediments)
related to facilitating cross-regional Black networking (Pan-Africanism) and explains the
rationale for Africa and its Diaspora to become reciprocal resources for each other.

1. Social Science / Ethnic Studies / African American Studies – Adult Literature
2. Business & Economics / General – Adult Literature
3. Technology / General – Adult Literature

Print information available on the last page.

This book is printed on acid-free paper.

To those dedicated to the betterment of Africa, its children and its resource use ... and thus, to the advancement of human civilization.

Nguzo moja haijengi nyumba.
(One pillar is not sufficient to build a house.)

Swahili proverb.

Contents

Contents

Preface

Africa is both the human homeland and the Earth's foremost resource-rich continent. These contexts and an associated analysis provide a conduit for understanding how the Continent became imperiled during the infamous African slave trade, the major catalyst for the half-millennium diaspora and populating of Black people throughout the Americas, Caribbean and Middle East. Historically, the descendants of those forcibly transported by ship from Africa across oceans to lifelong bondage/servitude in these plantation lands had come to be known as the African Diaspora; however, in recent times (from the 1960s through the present 21st century), voluntary migrants from Africa have relocated mainly to the United States, Canada and the EU countries, thus expanding the Diaspora's definition, size, and geopolitical scope.

UWENZI: *The Pan-African Factor, A 21st-Century View* seeks to facilitate a much-needed and provocative 21st-century dialogue on optimizing the linkage, networking and appreciation of African peoples, resources, culture and/or interests (commercial or otherwise) across regions, oceans and continents.—i.e., the *"Pan-African Factor"* (or more commonly, Pan-Africanism). As a focus point, the book emphasizes the pragmatism and rationale of developing strategies for Africa and its associated Diaspora (particularly the African American component) to be reciprocal resources for each other; this two-way interface is advanced as a conduit for building empowerment leverage and multilevel advancement (socio-cultural, political and economic). Also, selected impediments to Pan-African initiatives and development such as tribalism are outlined, and associated corrective tools like resource management/analysis, transformative education, conflict resolution efforts and other strategies are proposed to foster networking, new thinking, and linkages.

The book is a metamorphosis of a paper "A Contextual Outline and Analysis of 21st-Century Pan-Africanism" presented at the 3rd Biennial Kwame Nkrumah International Conference (August 22-24, 2014; Richmond Campus of Kwantlen Polytechnic University (Vancouver, BC, Canada)). The associated author team participated in the Conference via Blue Jeans (videoconferencing technology). Subsequent text additives and format modifications have been incorporated into the article-to-book conversion process.

UWENZI, the book's title, is written in Matisse ITC, a 1996-released Microsoft font. Matisse ITC is named in memory and commemoration of famous French artist Henri Matisse (1869-1954), whose works in the Modernist Art genre were greatly influenced by the angularity of African sculpture/art, with its extreme contrasts from flat areas to protruding surfaces. Its design-style, first created as a set of letter cut-outs by font designer Gregory Gray in 1995, attempts to capture Matisse's interpretation of African art. The word uwenzi (oo-wane-zee) is a KiSwahili term for cooperation, a pillar concept both culminating this work's tri-authored effort and underlying Pan-Africanism in reference to the global distribution, linkage and ancestral connectedness of African peoples. That philosophy is embodied metaphorically in the book's giraffe cover image which is bordered with Kuba Cloth, a Congo textile made from raffia palm leaves. When a giraffe herd drinks at a water hole, graze or rest somewhere, some of its members act as sentries and lookouts for the group, watching out for lions, hyenas and other predators— an act characteristic of teamwork and networking; often other herbivores such as zebras and impalas are attracted to the vicinity for similar needs because the congregation area is deemed safe as long as the giraffes do not suddenly flee—a sign that no danger has been spotted. Also, giraffes, 16–20 feet tall at maturation, have an elongated body with long neck and legs, keen eyesight, and large eyes located at the side of the head—all of which work in tandem to enable accurate, long-distance, panoramic vision from an elevated position. This book uses the *big picture* idea to discuss the **Pan-African Factor** from the perspective of 21st-century insight and analysis.

African Diaspora, An Introduction

Over the centuries, at least an estimated 30 million African slaves, mostly of wide-spanning Bantu cultures, were removed from the Continent's East and West coasts collectively for ocean vessel transport to the Americas, Middle East, or Asia; additional millions were captured and internally marched and traded along and across trans-Sahara networks in route to slave territories, markets and/or ports in North Africa. The major objective of this forced exodus was to expropriate Africa's resources (human and material), making the Caucasian world rich and creating a permanent, servile race. The time is both opportune and critical at this point in the 21st century for African people to engage in a rebuilding of self and culture, and to invest in resource optimization in order to reverse the ill effects of slavery, racism, colonialism and the resulting decline. To this end, it is worthwhile to take a journey back to the origins of the problem, before looking forward to solutions.

Scientific literature generally acknowledges the vicinity of modern-day Tanzania as the birthplace of hominids (ancestors of *homo sapiens*) and thus the homeland for modern humans, emerging about 200,000 years ago (Harmon, 2011; Rincon, 2003); however, some research posits the modern-day Cameroon area (Barras, 2013) or the Angola-Namibia borderland (Wade, 2009) as a likely site. Regardless which of the aforementioned sites is opined to be the human homeland, research consensus, according to genetic studies

4

and archaeological data, validates the African continent as the place, and by extension confirms the earliest humans as being Black people, the primordial DNA model for the human species. From whatever origination point—most likely Tanzania or some other relatively nearby East African location—humans eventually dispersed to all other parts of the Continent. Researchers say that small bands of these early humans steadily migrated out of Africa at least 60,000 years ago to eventually populate Asia, Europe and the rest of the globe; some also point to an earlier exodus time at approximately 125,000 years ago (Harmon, 2011). A combination of genetics, diet, climate and other socio-environmental factors are thought to have impacted these migrations in producing the variety of human phenotypes present on today's Earth. Though all humans are the offspring of Africa despite contemporary ethnoracial classifications and distinctions, the discussion focus in this work centers on the current networking and bonding efforts of the descendants of Africans who did not migrate out of the Continent 125,000 years ago. People of the Bantu phenotype, ancestry and cultural heritage crystallize the image of the aforementioned focus group and represent Africa in the mind's eye of most contemporary humans. The term *Bantu* will be further discussed in later sections of the book.

Africa has a vast number of languages, estimated at approximately 2,000, with each tongue being connected to a particular and distinct people (Heine & Nurse, 2000, p.1). A major cultural weakness was and still is tribalism, exacerbated by an overkill of languages; this weakness led to mistrust, animosity, jealousies, endless squabbles amongst nations and eventually continual inter-ethnic friction; additionally, migrations induced by wars and environmental changes (volcano explosions, drought, desertification, etc.),during the course of hundreds of centuries, pushed new peoples into the territorial spaces of others, leading to increased ethnic conflicts, hatred, and violence over philosophies and resources (food, water, land, etc.). Prisoners of war and kidnap victims were taken captive and sold as slaves by rival groups (Wilson & Ayerst, 1976, p. 71); some were eventually absorbed into rival ethnicities.

A Pan-Africanist perspective and analysis, that is, a position and philosophy promoting cooperation and a common history/destiny amongst people of African descent, irrespective of ethnicity and geographical residence, attempts to network the stakeholders of Africa's future. Actually, because of the enormity and scope of the African slave trade in dispersing millions of people over a 1000-plus year period, Black people, whether residing in Africa or somewhere in the associated Diaspora, have scattered, unbeknownst, bloodline relatives living in various parts of the world. The term *Diaspora* as applied to Africa is used to collectively denote Black populations living outside of Africa, particularly those whose current geography is a resulting byproduct of the slave trade of centuries past. The historical African slave trade is the basic conduit that launched the perspective prism for the term "African Diaspora"; prior to the 1960s, the term was used largely to collectively group people currently living in the Americas, Caribbean, Middle East, and Europe who trace their ancestral entry there to enslaved people forcibly transported from Africa. Today, the context of discussing the African Diaspora has expanded to include Africans who voluntarily migrated to non-African nations a half century ago, especially those taking up residence in the US, Canada and the EU (European Union).

Unfortunately, in these ancient times, the spirit of Pan-Africanism (African networking and pan-cultural appreciation) didn't exist; thus, most groups could potentially be seen or perceived as the enemy of another. An important note here is the fact that in centuries past, ethnic groups (not just in Africa, but across the globe) did not generally see other ethnic groups who were of similar phenotype as necessarily being the same people; thus, a Mandingo was not a Maasai though both are African, any more than a Frenchman was an Italian though both are European. Therefore, regarding African participation in the capture and sale of slaves, most did not sell their own people into slavery, but sold mainly foreigners, that is, their perceived enemies. Most languages, across continents and cultures, historically regarded words for "foreigner" as synonyms for "enemy"; hence, *mgeni* (mmm-gay-nee), KiSwahili for "visitor," also means "stranger." In the Biblical context, the concept of neighbor was actually reserved for a trusted friend, an associate, or a familiar nearby resident (notably among farmers), not just any fellow human, as is theologically promoted today (particularly in Christianity). The term descends linguistically from the Old English word *neahgebur* (neah (near) + gebur (dweller)). Ironically, Arabs and Europeans, despite having internal squabbles between and amongst themselves, all agreed that Black people (Africans) were a slave race by divine edict, while African ethnicities generally saw each other as dissimilar strangers. John Speke, 19th-century British explorer of Africa and namesake for Speke's Gazelle (a type of East-Central African antelope), advocated the Curse of Ham Theory—the conjecture that Blacks, as progeny of the Biblical Noah's youngest son Ham, are cursed as perpetual slaves by God—and also founded the Hamitic Hypothesis, the notion that all civilization and culture in Central Africa were introduced by offshoot, sharper-featured, Caucasian tribes from Ethiopia (descendents of one of Ham's progeny), for example Tutsis and Wanyamwezi ... thus denoting "a people who are deemed more intelligent and civilized than the surrounding, *native Negroids*" (Garrett, 1997; East African Girl, 2012). According to this Israelite/Hebrew fable (appearing in the Book of Genesis), Ham made an egregious transgression against his father Noah; some spins identify *ridicule for drunken-induced nakedness or castration as* examples. Variants of the story of Noah and the transgression of Ham appear in the Abrahamic sacred texts, i.e., Torah (Judaism), Bible (Christianity), and Qu'ran (Islam). As the transgression's consequences, Noah, with the condoning of the God of Abraham, cursed Ham by turning his skin black and decreeing that his progeny would be forever slaves or menials to the seeds of his brothers Shem and Japheth. Many adherents (and associated scholars alike) of the Abrahamic faiths (Judaism, Christianity and Islam) have postulated that Africans, Asians and Caucasians (the denoted, major branches of humanity) are spawned respectively from Noah's three sons Ham, Shem and Japheth. In this fable narrative, Noah is generally presumed to be a Caucasian (or White in the common vernacular). For over 2,000 years, the nature of Ham's transgression and the reason for Canaan (Ham's immediate progeny) to bear the weight of the curse instead of Ham (Noah's transgressor) have been debated. The fable's original objective was to justify the subjection of the Canaanites to the Israelites, but in later centuries, the narrative was interpreted by Jews, Christians, and Muslims as an explanation for the enslavement and subjugation of African (Black) people. Canaanites, Midianites, Jebusites, Cushites, Ethiopians, and numerous other peoples mentioned in these aforementioned sacred texts are thought to be descended from Ham through the seed/lineage of his son Canaan; thus, the connection of Ham, his descendants' curse and Black people was woven and diabolically applied through varying interpretations, text translations and spins. Lingering and long-held theological beliefs have linked African heritage and dark skin with divine punishment, suffering and servitude to justify White supremacy (Caucasian advantage), mistreatment/abuse of Africans, and the perceived misfortunes of Africa as divine.

In continuing the discussion of African enslavement, Arabs came to Africa approximately fifteen hundred years ago looking for assets, wealth and business opportunities to supply their customer/clientele markets and needs, mainly in Arabic-speaking, Middle Eastern, and Asian nations; they sought ivory (elephant tusks), male slaves as tusk "donkeys," eunuchs to serve as harem guards, soldiers or homosexual toys (Levi, 2010), women as concubines (sex slaves), and children as pedophilic commodities and eventual plug-ins to aforementioned adult duties (Stuart-Mogg, 2010, pp. 24–25). Five hundred years ago Europeans also came for resources: natural materials such as ivory (for piano keys, combs, billiard balls, dominoes, and other products), gold, spices, and timber, but mainly adult slaves to build new colonies (US, Brazil, Haiti, Jamaica, etc.) and maintain associated agricultural plantations. They also enslaved children as future breeders of more laborers. Both groups warred and collaborated with each other in the process of acquiring Africa's resources, mainly slaves and ivory (Conniff, 1987). Some African kingdoms (e.g., Wanyamwezi, Yao, Fulani, Ashanti, and Dahomey, just to name a few) secured ivory and slaves for sale to Arabs and Europeans in exchange for rum, guns, cloth, beads and other trinkets, thereby making Africa vulnerable to centuries of exploitation, civil collapse, and resource mismanagement.

Caucasian-based literature and race theories framing Africans as slaves by divine edict, and as evil, savage, ugly, and childlike, have worked in tandem with apartheid and other efforts to subjugate Blacks as inferiors vis-à-vis White society (Hood, 1994, pp. 9–10; Keane, 1995, pp. 13–14). For example, Leviticus 21:18 (KJV) points out that those with flat noses (common Black physical features) are unworthy and unwelcome in the sight and presence of God.

The European and Arab slave trades were the catalyst for the transport of millions of Blacks, primarily peoples of Bantu linguistic and cultural heritage, from Africa across the globe via the Atlantic and Indian Oceans to the Americas, the Caribbean, Europe, Asia, and the Middle East. Famous Africa explorer and Scottish physician David Livingstone, a slavery abolitionist, estimated that only one in five persons survived the *interior capture point-to-coast* trek process due to horrendous conditions of squalor, hunger, disease, fatigue, beatings, and other maladies (Conniff, 1987). Whole territories had

been significantly depopulated due to slave capture-and-removal operations without even a full population recovery today, as in present-day Chad and the Central African Republic. The ivory trade was a major factor in this decimation.

This slave coffle image/engraving (captioned as **"Slavers Revenging Their Losses"**) is based upon a sketch done by explorer David Livingstone (Waller, 1874, p.62). The drawing, shown/listed on www.slaveryimages.org as "Slave Coffle, East Africa, 1866" (Image Reference C014), was compiled by Jerome Handler and Michael Tuite and was sponsored by the Virginia Foundation for the Humanities and the University of Virginia Library.

Ivory and slaves were inseparable; for every tusk, there was to be the capture/purchase of one African slave as a transport "donkey." Africans, chained by goree sticks (forked neck harnesses) in a caravan, would carry tusks weighing up to 65 pounds (and sometimes heavier) along an *interior-to-coast* trek, a distance sometimes extending from 300 to 1,000 miles; this method of bundled shackling is called a coffle, *a line of animals, prisoners or slaves chained and*

Ivory Tusks

This photo, taken in Kenya and featured on the 2012-2014 Tsavo Trust website, captures the diversity of African elephant tusks in size and shape. It also offers a sobering, contextual glimpse into the arduous task of carrying ivory tusks, as endured by African slaves in pre-21st-century Arab coffle caravans.

driven along together. Most of the bearers died of malnutrition and exhaustion-related illnesses by journey's end. Henry Morton Stanley, 19th-century Anglo-American explorer, once wrote that every pound of ivory "has cost the life of one man, woman, or child" in Africa (Conniff, 1987). The ivory trade's toll on human life was massive. In the late 1890s, for example, Pratt, Read, & Co., a major ivory-product manufacturer from Deep River, CT, alone was cutting 12,000 pounds of ivory monthly to supply what amounted to national piano mania in the US (Conniff, 1987); using the above equation, 12,000 Africans would have perished each month to supply that company's ivory cache.

Many African leaders (e.g., Mwinyi Dugumbi; Bwana Nzige; Mirambo; Mtagamoyo) from varying groups and kingdoms, and their cronies particularly Black, mercenary slaving gangs known as *ruga ruga* were happy to sell off lots of people to Arabs and Europeans in exchange for guns, worthless beads, new trade connections, and the promise of special favors (Smith, 2009). These traded or enslaved persons included: captured people from rival or militarily weaker ethnic groups; community members who were disliked (uppity family members, dissidents, criminals, and the trifling); and debt-payoff pawns. African involvement was intricate and very significant; this participation ranged in scope and took many forms: capturing others; providing canoes to slavers for transport through interior waterways (Farrant, 1975, p. 83); allowing territorial passage of slave caravans; and providing armed security details for slave caravans, just to name a few. However, not all African nations participated in the slave network. Some fought against the slavers; subsequently, non-participating groups always had to defend themselves against slavers. Conflict, chaos, and vicious brutality always loomed around the corner as a common occurrence, making large spaces in Africa probable areas for one to be captured either by slavers or groups participating in the slaving network (Farrant, 1975, p. 125).

Recall an 1882 encounter and conversation in the East African interior by British missionary, explorer and mariner Alfred Swann with one of the headmen for Hamed bin Muhammed's slave caravan; Swann was a slavery abolitionist in similar mold to David Livingstone. Hamed bin Muhammad, a Black Arab nicknamed and infamously known as Tippu Tip, was a ruthless slave trader, plunderer and mass murderer. This (unnamed) headman encountered by Swann could have been an Arab or a Black man—the text account does not say which, in this instance, though many in such a capacity were Islamic Blacks who identified themselves as Arabs and subscribed to the notion that Africans are naturally inferior and servile. At the time, Swann was on expedition and business, courtesy of the London Missionary Society; the conversation epitomizes a dialogue between two colonialists and businessmen—one, a Christian, and the other, a Muslim. In this quotation excerpt, the encounter went as follows:

> As they filed past, we noticed many chained by the neck. Others had their necks fastened at the forks of poles about six feet long, the ends of which were supported by the men who preceded them. The women, who were as numerous as the men, carried babies on their backs in addition to a tusk of ivory or other burden on their heads. They looked at us with suspicion and fear, having been told, as we subsequently ascertained, that White men always desired to release slaves in order to eat their flesh, like the Upper Congo cannibals. It is difficult adequately to describe the filthy state of their bodies; in many instances, not only scarred by the cut of a chikote (raw-hide whip)... but feet and shoulders were a mass of sores, made more painful by the swarms of flies which followed the march and lived on the flowing blood. They presented a moving picture

of utter misery, and one could not help wondering how any of them had survived the long trek from the Upper Congo, at least a 1,000 miles distant ... The headmen in charge were most polite to us, as they passed our camp ... Addressing one, I pointed out that many of the slaves were unfit to carry loads. To this he smilingly replied: "They have no choice! They must go, or die!" "Are all these slaves destined for Zanzibar?" (says Swann) "Most of them, the remainder will stay at the coast." (says the Arab) "Have you lost many on the road?" (says Swann) "Yes! Numbers have died of hunger!" (says the Arab) "Any run away?" (says Swann) "No, they are too well guarded. Only those who become possessed with the devil try to escape; there is nowhere they could run to if they should go." (says the Arab) "What do you do when they become too ill to travel?" (says Swann) "Spear them at once! ... For if we did not, others would pretend they were ill in order to avoid carrying their loads. No! We never leave them alive on the road; they all know our custom." (says the Arab) "I see women carrying not only a child on their backs, but, in addition, a tusk of ivory or other burden on their heads. What do you do in their case when they become too weak to carry both child and ivory? Who carries the ivory?" (says Swann) "She does! We cannot leave valuable ivory on the road. We spear the child and make her burden lighter. (says the Arab) Ivory first, child afterwards!" (says the Arab) Swann raged: "Ivory! Always ivory! What a curse the elephant has been to Africans. By himself, the slave did not pay to transport; but, plus ivory he was a paying game." (Meredith, 2001, pp. 84–85)

The just-mentioned conversation, which appears in numerous books on the East African slave trade, underscores the fact that Africa was perceived as *ripe for the taking* by outsiders/interlopers having

varied interests there. Arabs and Europeans warred and collaborated with each other in the process of acquiring ivory, slaves, and other African resources. European enslavement of the African ended in the mid-19th-century in

This wooden yoke photo (originally captioned as **"A Method of Securing Slaves"**) is an 1882 picture taken by missionary Alfred J. Swann as he witnessed an Arab slave caravan in Tanganyika (East Africa) (Swann, 1910, p.51). The picture, shown/listed on www.slaveryimages.org as "Wooden Yoke Used in Coffle, East Africa, 1882" (Image Reference *Swann*), was compiled by Jerome Handler and Michael Tuite and was sponsored by the Virginia Foundation for the Humanities and the University of Virginia Library.

the wake of philosophical debates about the contradiction of Christianity and slavery, while the majority of the Arab slave trade fizzled out during the early 20th century mainly as a consequence of aggressive European colonial and anti-slaving efforts on African soil.

Afterwards, legal African servitude was replaced with colonialism and/or apartheid until the 1960s; however, White-minority rule and associated, legal apartheid remained in Zimbabwe and South Africa until 1980 and the early 1990s, respectively. Resources, both human and material, have been drained as a consequence; vast, natural wealth and resources (diamonds, oil, coltan, uranium, just to name a few) position Africa to be deemed as ripe for siege and conquest, today no less than yesterday. As a consequence of colonial exploitation and administrative ineptness and resource abuse by indigenous leadership, the Continent is in a state of rebuilding.

Issues and Initiatives of Pan-Africanism

Long ago, Africa and its peoples created and introduced the world to the basic disciplines of human knowledge: mathematics, medicine, logic, ethics, advanced architecture, etc. (Katembo, B., 2012, p. 1); today, its associated civilizations have fallen in economic and technical productivity, but can be retooled and rebuilt, as some bright spots like Rwanda, Botswana, Zambia, Seychelles and Namibia currently demonstrate. All civilizations reach levels of peaks and valleys, with Africa being no exception. There are, however, numerous bright spots taking place in Africa, with the following as examples: development of the East African Community (EAC), a geopolitical confederation of five nations (Kenya, Tanzania, Uganda, Rwanda, and Burundi) sharing ideas, resources, language and culture; manufacture and testing of an electric car at Makarere University (Uganda) made from use of local/indigenous technology and materials in 2011 (Kavuma, 2011); continued research at Makarere University on using local Ugandan mosquito-eating plants as a tool to reduce malaria-infection levels (Womakuyu, 2010); good governance (resource management; administration) in Botswana; and positive economic growth and development in post-genocide Rwanda. In today's integrated, global and postcolonial world, African people on the Continent and in the Diaspora would be prudent to explore new strategies for empowerment and rethink old ones.

Slavery, from 1,500 years prior to and through the early 20th century, and colonization, from the late 19th century to the 1960s, have socialized significant sectors of Black people toward victimization, poor self-image, and counterproductive views such as, "Africa is a savage place, having contributed little to the progress of humanity and civilization." Treatment and therapy are needed as cures to these social maladies in parallel to the continued vigilance and push-back efforts against systemic racism, particularly as noted within the US socio-cultural landscape. Some additional effects of these ailments on Continental Africans and African Americans are: poor management skills regarding the running of institutions, for example, HBCUs; repressive African governments; perpetual war, political/economic decay, chaos and famine in numerous African countries (e.g., Zimbabwe); slave mentality; lack of desire toward academics and self-drive in general; victimization mindset; destruction of root culture; inter-group hostility and curmudgeonly attitudes; dysfunctional family structures with absentee fathers and poor parenting; tension-filled male–female relationships; overall non-competitiveness within a robust society except in the arenas of entertainment such as music and sports; and self-rejection of African physical features (Fihlani, 2013; Moore, 2009), for example the international craze by Black women to buy and use skin-lightening creams (Msasanuri, 2009). Unless the aforementioned ailments are remedied, global vulnerability of Black people to oppression, racism and social decay will intensify.

Resources (Management and Mismanagement)

Today, as a result of the damage done by the slave trade, colonialism and wars, and the self-infliction of poor leadership and resource mismanagement, Africa, though rich in natural resources, has fallen from its pinnacle and ancient greatness to a level of impoverishment, politically fragility, and economic instability ... a continent gripped by war, famine, tribalism and corrupt brutal governments which egregiously abuse and squander human capital and physical materials, e.g., Burundi crisis (Aljazeera Staff Writer, 2016). African people, and the African continent as a geopolitical entity, should harness, cultivate and wisely use resources for survival.

Resources are tools which assist in the fruition and/or completion of any initiative. They may be categorized as hard, tangible (e.g., minerals, water, land, technological innovations, money, etc.) or soft, intangible (e.g., problem-solving/analysis, management skills, language, intuitive vision, culture, technology, etc.). In Africa's case, resources are vast and abundant, particularly hard/natural resources, though most must be better cultivated and better managed to optimize benefit to the Continent's people, both in Africa and in the Diaspora (British Pathé Series Reporter, 2014; Even At The Doors Reporter, 2013). Africa, as a metaphor and as a single, conceptual resource entity, basically represents the fabled King Solomon's Mines; it is from this resource treasure that much of the world depends for development and sustenance.

While Africa's socio-political issues independently affect poverty and poverty reduction, it is easiest to see their impact when we speak about the resource dilemma. Resource endowments—such as coltan, diamonds, oil, gas, and hardwoods—can become a source for financial mismanagement in the face of the political incentives and policy failures they generate (Acemoglu & Robinson, 2004). In these circumstances, policy failure is the prime cause of the underperformance of the resource-abundant countries (Lal & Myint, 1996). Since these resources are commonly owned by the state, it is incumbent upon the government to decide the extraction level, timeframe, and expenditure of the rents. This government monopoly gives the governments the privilege to maximize the profits at the expense of the proletariat. It is easy to see that some governments would wish to benefit economically and politically from the resource as quickly as possible, which leads to over-extraction and short-term policymaking. Furthermore, the wealth these resources produce for the state heightens political competition, and the ruling party may well be driven to use these resources to maintain and expand its influence. Offering public-sector contracts and employment is one of the key patronage mechanisms available in such states, and there is evidence that resource-rich countries with stagnant economies have an over expanded state (Auty, 1998). For instance, in copper-rich Zambia, between 1966 and 1980 the average yearly growth rate in public sector employment was 7.2 percent, while private employment on average contracted by 6.2 percent each year (Gelb, Knight & Sabot, 1991).

How the government chooses to invest and spend resources is often influenced by the quality of their state institutions. Institutions that are competent, transparent, and accountable are able to manage resources in a manner that is separated from patrimonial practices, and they are allocated according to rational and independent criteria. Even as poverty increased, President Frederick Chiluba's illicit earnings, for instance, were funneled through non-transparent, "secret" security and presidential accounts that profited from Zambia's state-owned copper mines. On the other hand, Botswana's success in managing its diamond wealth has been attributed to its "good governance" and in particular its stable institutions (Handley et al., 2009).

In particular, voice and accountability, government effectiveness, market-friendly policies and regulatory frameworks, and effective anti-corruption measures have had the most impact. Generally then, poor governance, rights abuse, corruption, clientelism and other "informal" practices combine with structural constraints to generate and maintain poverty. They also make it difficult for people to initiate and carry through reforms that would improve their livelihoods. It is for this reason that Western development specialists tackle poverty on two levels: at one level by attempting to strengthen economic development and growth, and at the other by improving local and national governance. Both strategies focus on putting into place or reforming state and social institutions (Handley et al., 2009).

Pan-Africanist Education

Thus far in the 21st century, education is perhaps the single most important issue facing Africans because true education, that is, education based on indigenous African practices and customs, breaks the current cycle of dependence and the lethal consumption of systematic White supremacy and hegemony for future generations. Evidence of the value of supporting education to achieve development is convincing. A more equitable distribution of education correlates with reduced economic poverty and inequality and faster economic growth (Birdsall & Londoño, 1997). Education for girls has positive impacts on women's empowerment and lowers women's risk of being poor. It also generates indirect benefits in terms of the health of their infants and children, family nutrition, immunization rates, and educational attainment for their children (Bruns, Mingat & Rakotomalala, 2003). It has been found in Africa that education for boys and girls may be the single most effective weapon against HIV/AIDS (Bruns, Mingat & Rakotomalala, 2003). Primary education also contributes to improved natural resource management. Education, especially at the secondary and tertiary levels, is fundamental for the construction of democratic societies and globally competitive economies. In short, education is a powerful instrument for reducing inequality and poverty and for laying the foundations for sustained economic growth, effective institutions and sound governance (Bruns, Mingat & Rakotomalala, 2003).

One problem with the global White supremacist educational system is that education itself does not seem to be its focal point. That is, learning the 3Rs does not seem to be its true aim. The US educational system is based on a Prussian (German) model, and the aim of that system was to "instill social obedience in the citizens through indoctrination" (Melton, 1988). Evidence that the US system is designed to create such citizens is so clear it is virtually invisible to the eye because minds trained in the system are so indoctrinated. The US educational system uses a form of "schizophrenic chaos" to ensure status quo maintenance. To explain, the system operates under the ultimate control of legislators who are most often entrenched into the fabric of the American aristocracy. In one decade the aristocrats advocate for phonetic approaches in language learning and in another decade they advocate for whole-language approaches. The two approaches to learning oppose one another—the former focuses upon having children learn the technical aspects for language acquisition and mastery of concepts, while the latter begets acquisition and mastery based on figuring out the meaning of things. It would make sense to teach both simultaneously, but employment maintenance for teachers will be predicated upon "mastery teaching" of one or the other at a given time. Hence, in the time a teacher would need to gain true mastery of either approach, the approach has become irrelevant and they have switched to some other thing.

It is important to note that phonetic and whole-language approaches are merely examples of the reigning behavior within the educational system. To take another example, Owen (1985) unveils the duplicitous nature of the system in revealing that the SAT test is only effective when some students score well and others do not. In other words, some failure is mandatory for proper system functioning. Owen's research reveals that the "correlation between SAT scores and college grades [is] lower than the correlation between weight and height; in other words you would have a better chance of predicting a person's height by looking at his weight than you would of predicting his freshman grades by looking only at his/her SAT scores" (p. 207). While many university admissions offices will claim that SATs are only one measure used among many, considering Owen's findings, why are they still being used at all? Because using them ensures maintenance of the status quo—especially since the tests are periodically changed. Somehow the changes always reify the status quo—the "achievement gap." Another example of the education system's audaciously incorrigible behavior is that after decades of attempting to change basic curriculum misnomers such as the notion that "Christopher Columbus discovered America," that falsehood is still taught in classrooms every day in the US. In sum, maintenance of the status quo is ensured by using pseudo-novelty, methods that are proven to be useless, and omissions and commissions that successfully protect the status quo. The result of such a systematic malady is a schizophrenic system that appears evolutionary but is as regressive as it is guileful.

African children in the system. All children in the system. In the US, African children suffer the most. Many African scholars (from the continent of Africa and around the globe) are calling for an African-centered Pan-Africanist education that is reminiscent of indigenous African cultural practices and beliefs (Akoto, 1992; Hilliard, 1998; Kumah-Abiwu, 2016). Over the past 20 years or so, there have been lively debates about whether or not indigenous African education existed (Howe, 1998; Lefkowitz, 1996). Often at the center of such debates is a dehumanizing "question" about whether or not Islam and the West brought the only "true education" to Africa.

Dignifying such blatant ignorance and racism with a response is not the goal here. Suffice it to say that without education one cannot produce such productive humans as Kandake, Prempeh, Hannibal, Amenemhat, Imhotep, Nzingha, Shptabra and countless others. Without education one could not have built the University of Ipetlsut, or the University at Sankore at Timbuktu, which was the world learning center of its time. Without education it would not be possible to sustain and develop the world's oldest people. Finally, there is a reason why famous philosophers such as Socrates believed it to be to his benefit to be taught by African teachers (Asante, 2000). The question of whether or not indigenous African education existed is not up for debate. It would be like trying to prove that most of the earth's surface is water to someone who refuses to believe it, regardless of evidence. Considering the vestiges of colonialism that remain in Africa, and the all-encompassing presence of worldwide white supremacy (Cress-Welsing, 1991), the education that most African children receive is under the ultimate control of Europeans. Europeans as a composite group, and especially powerful Europeans, have both historically and in the present day found it reasonable to question the true humanity of African people (Watkins, 2007). The highly respected German philosopher Hegel captures the essence of White supremacy in his famous 1831 quote:

> "At this point we leave Africa, not to mention it again. For it is no historical part of the World; it has no movement or development to exhibit. Historical movements in it—that is in its northern part—belong to the Asiatic or European World. Carthage displayed there an important transitory phase of civilization; but, as a Phoenician colony, it belongs to Asia. Egypt will be considered in reference to the passage of the

human mind from its Eastern to its Western phase, but it does not belong to the African Spirit. What we properly understand by Africa, is the Unhistorical, Undeveloped Spirit, still involved in the conditions of mere nature, and which had to be presented here only as on the threshold of the World's History." (Hegel, 1956, p. 99)

While the boldness is sometimes lessened, the ideas have remained the same as represented in 2007 by Nobel Prize-winning scientist James Watson, who stated that "[I am] inherently gloomy about the prospect of Africa [because] all our social policies are based on the fact that their intelligence is the same as ours—whereas all the testing says not really."

African children worldwide are under the ultimate control of a system that has a Hegelian and "Watsonian" consciousness. In that system, African children learn virtually no positive things about themselves as a Pan-African group. As a result, many of them develop negative ideas about themselves (Wilson, 1993) and wish to be seen as being different from their group. Hence, the goals of Pan-Africanism are made extraordinarily more difficult. That is, African people themselves are being reared from the beginning of their lives to be in the first line of defense against Pan-Africanism.

The critical need for recovery and rescue: precursors to Pan-Africanism. Pan-Africanism refers to the historical and cultural connection Africans have to one another, regardless of present geographical residence. That is, one of Pan-Africanism's core tenets argues that all people of African descent are, in fact, Africans. The educational system, which is White supremacist in nature, has positioned itself as a major competitor to Pan-Africanism by advocating instead that Black children are "Black Americans" or "Jamaican Americans" or "Black Brazilians" or representative of such labels as the "Hip Hop Generation", "Youth Culture" and "Pop Culture." The aforementioned nomenclatures represent small pieces of what becomes the content of White supremacist miseducation. Those small pieces represent larger ideas that relate to dislocated identity and misplaced allegiance. African youth are miseducated to believe, for example, that they are Jamaican and they should be proud to be Jamaican for whatever reason. Or that they should be a proud Black Brazilian because of their accomplishments in Brazil. The same is true for Africans in the US, Europe, the Caribbean and so forth. A Pan-Africanist sentiment would mean that our youth are taught to have primary allegiance to Africa, not Jamaica, Brazil, and so on. What is required in order to get to the Pan-Africanist sentiment is an African-centered education. Offering an African education (as opposed to an African-centered one) would mean using the tools, contents and techniques used by Africans prior to European/Arabic/Islamic/Christian/Asian invasions to teach and reach African children. An African "centered" education takes those tools, contents and techniques into account, but also adds other critical elements such as Black Nationalist sentiment, re-Africanization, and culturally relevant pedagogy (Shockley, 2007; Shockley & Frederick, 2010).

It makes sense that when Africans educated themselves prior to invasions, they did so without having to consider outside cultural influences. When Black Nationalism, the re-Africanization movement and culturally relevant pedagogy attach to indigenous African cultural offerings, African-centered education is produced. African-centered education is the act of placing the needs and interests of the Black community at the center of the Black child's education. More specifically, the practice of African-centered education requires internalization of African-centered education constructs (Shockley, 2007) such as recognizing the African identity of the Black child, internalizing Pan-Africanism, adopting African culture into one's life; it is also the "total use of method to effect the psychological, cultural, and economic conditions in the Black community" through education (Asante, 1998, p. 4) and it is the use of "culturally relevant pedagogy" in order to effectively teach and reach Black children (Ladson-Billings, 2001). Asante (1998) argues that:

> [African-centered education] seeks to understand [phenomena] by beginning all analysis from the African person as human agent. In classes, it means that the African American child must be connected, grounded to information presented in the same way White children are grounded when we discuss literature, history, mathematics, and science. Teachers who do not know this information with respect to Africans must seek it out from those who do know it. Afrocentrists do not take anything away from White history, except its aggressive urge to pose as universal. (p. 16)

As stated before, African-centered education consists of numerous constructs and is almost a "minimum prerequisite" for what many African-centered educationists call "re-Africanization."

Re-Africanization. Re-Africanization is a conscious attempt to reconnect with the African past. Akoto and Akoto (1999) suggest that the African person (child) must rediscover his/her African self, redefine what it means to be a person within the African Diaspora, and participate in the revitalization of the African world (p. 8). Re-Africanization eventuates in nation building—the literal attempt to build the Black community via the creation of functioning families. Added together, an African-centered education requires that educators consume the constructs of African-centered education, and understand that the approach affects the whole child. It is not just about academics, and within classrooms everything that is presented to children must be relevant to the needs of the community; that is, there is no knowledge for knowledge's sake. Finally, the overall purpose of education, from an African-centered perspective, is to bring African children to the point of replacing colonial/enslaved ideas about identity with African-derived notions. Organic replacements would mark significant advancements in the mission to recover and rescue African people and their progeny. And again, such replacements are precursors to imbuing African children with a Pan-Africanist sentiment.

In an "education sense," Pan-Africanism is less a practice than it is a belief and/or a sentiment. From an African-centered perspective, a teacher teaches "who s/he is." In other words, documents such as curricula and other pedagogical materials are almost unimportant compared to schema of understandings already existent within the teacher (Shockley, Bond & Rollins, 2008). What we have begun to understand in teacher education is that the kindergarten through baccalaureate degree experience, in addition to the other White supremacist-based learning that a person takes on in life, is the powerful force that determines what the teacher will transmit to students in a classroom. So in that sense, a sentiment of "Pan-Europeanism", i.e., Caucasian cooperation and networking, is transmitted to all students all day every day in virtually every place in the world—often under the euphemisms "the West," "Capitalism," "American," "progressive," "modern," "English," and so on. Though transforming into a melting pot in the 21st century, the United States in a historical sense probably represents the greatest example of Caucasian achievement in ethnic distinctions like English, German, Irish and French being discouraged and White cooperation being emphasized. Since White supremacy operates via rhetorical ethics and dishonesty, Pan-Europeanist sentiment becomes ideological; for example with statements such as "we are all the same," or "race does not matter." When such statements are made, the reality of difference and the fact that race does in fact matter become rhetoric which must not be spoken of, ever. Changing what students get in classrooms requires that the people teaching them change their mental schemata. Hence, Pan-Africanist sentiment will only become normalized among a critical mass of Africans across the globe when the teachers of African children change their schemata from being Eurocentric to being African-centered. African-centeredness among a critical mass of people resolves the identity crisis. Once that crisis is resolved, the oneness of who African people are becomes apparent.

For Black children worldwide, the critical element needing to be extracted from Pan-Africanism relates to culture. What has become necessary is that Africans reconnect with who we were the last time we were sovereign, unencumbered by outside influence. Pan-Africanist goals will not be reached until more intentional effort goes into changing what is happening in schools. Unfortunately many people overlook the critical need for a deeper understanding of what education is. As Anwisye (2009) explains,

> Education is more than the 3Rs. Simply being employment- or entrepreneurship-ready, drug-free, gang-free, unpregnant out-of-wedlock, and "proud of our heritage," is not enough. Education is a lifelong womb-to-the-tomb process, which in all nations and cultures is designed to instill a sense of allegiance to the nation/culture and to equip its members or citizens with the will, skills, desire and commitment necessary to advance that nation/culture and to secure or maintain its freedom. (p.1)

Pan-Africanist sovereignty-based education would mean learning for a purpose. Breasted (1937) clarifies that African education has always been about learning with a purpose:

> "Learning possessed but one aspect for the Egyptian, namely: its practical usefulness. An ideal pleasure in the search for truth, the pursuit of science for its own sake, were unknown to him. The learned equipment was an advantage which lifted a youth above all other classes ... and for that reason, the boy must be early put into the school and diligently kept to his tasks." (pp. 98–99)

Hence, indigenously speaking, for Africans as a composite group, learning has been about preparing young people to "take control of the psychic and physical spaces that [Africans] call their own" (Akoto, 1999). In many cases, young people were taught to do things as they were in the midst of doing them and/or when they had a responsibility for doing something. Being taught was not an exercise in memorization, but instead planning for life lessons and learning how to do practical things. Chants, songs, dances, call-and-response, storytelling, and plays have been important indigenous methods for teaching and reaching the children. Enculturation is critical and happens systematically. One does not simply raise children. There are traditions such as chants and songs that are important in the enculturation process. Fu-Kiau (2001) pointed out that many of the processes used to work with children even have names, such as "Kindezi," which refers to the Bantu art of babysitting and child rearing.

A critical aspect of educating youth comes via rites of passage and initiation. Mbiti (1992) reveals how Africans enculturated youth:

"[The] initiates rehearse adult life: boys go hunting with miniature bows and arrows, and girls cut small twigs (which symbolize firewood for the home). Late the same day the original operators at the first ceremony spit beer over the candidates to bless them, and the children return to their "home" in the bush. Here they must overcome objects that are placed before them. Each boy is given a special stick, which he must retain; and that evening a dance for the initiates takes place. With their special sticks the boys perform symbolic sexual acts upon the girls; and on the following day, they are examined on the meaning of riddles and puzzles carved on the sticks or drawn on sand. Afterwards the boys fetch sugar-canes, this being a form of permitted "stealing" acceptable and necessary for that particular purpose; and with the sugar-cane they make beer for their incumbents." (p. 119)

What would be optimal is re-Africanization that leads to African-centered schools which foster a sense of Pan-Africanism in African youth. It is telling that one of the first questions would be "how do we gain access to your youth?" Who does have access to African youth? The answer is whoever has been able to indoctrinate them away from Pan-Africanism and African-centeredness. African people have a major predicament - that is, the adults do not have ready access to the youth because, in the US, the system of White supremacy has intentionally created that circumstance. In places such as Africa and the Caribbean, the White supremacist system may not control the daily happenings so closely, but the daily happenings are indeed monitored and controlled financially. Because the so-called education system and the media have created, even within the body of African youth, White supremacist Pan-Europeanists, efforts to engage the youth in African-centered/Pan-Africanist ways are quite difficult. If accessing them is difficult, imagine the difficulty of attempting to use the formal educational system to teach them in new ways. The system has responded to 1960s types of efforts to engage African youth by upping its mental indoctrination campaign so much so that the first line of defense against Pan-Africanism is the youth themselves.

Considering the realities discussed above, perhaps the best course of action is the kind of steps that are being taken by African-centered school leaders across the country. They are implementing rites of passage programs and initiation rituals outside of formal school hours. Another solution that many Africans are now considering is African community home schools. Community home schools are established via understandings between parents within a given community. One or more of the parents (often with an education background) organizes educational experiences for the children. Those experiences are based upon African culture and organizing principles. The parents in the community pay fees to the teacher who is organizing the experiences for the children. Adults in such communities are continuously engaged in a process of re-Africanization.

One of the reasons why African community schools are being established is that African-centered schools are quite difficult to maintain. In order to maintain a school that goes against the European world cultural thrust, the community must support it. It is difficult to imagine how a community under pressure from the system to assimilate would maintain its composure enough to support institutions/missions that every day they are being taught to separate from. Hence, African community home schools have become the best option in the quest to eventually get to Pan-Africanism.

Impediments to Pan-Africanism

Tribalism

A *tribe* is thought of as a group of people who are descended from common ancestors and ruled by a hereditary "chief," who share a single culture (including, in particular, language and religion), and who live in a well-defined geographical region (Appiah, 1999, p. 703). Tribalism is most-often conceptually characterized as intense inter-ethnic mistrust, agitation and rivalry, usually leading to sustained hatred, (violent) conflict or warfare. Though significant, it connoted as the primary cause for lack of economic progress in Africa underestimates the complexity of African societies and politics, and diverts policymakers' attention from the real causes of underdevelopment. The African reality has been defined by the ideology of tribalism. However, European colonialism, like any epoch, is responsible for bringing the new order of reconstructing this African reality. As Mafeje notes:

> "In many instances the colonial authorities helped to create the things called "tribes," in the sense of political communities; this process coincided with and was helped along by the anthropologists' preoccupation with "tribes." This provided the material as well as the ideological base of what is now called "tribalism." (Mafeje, 1971, p. 254).

Tribalism as an inseparable African custom and concept has been largely promoted by anthropologists. The field of anthropology, by tradition, is still "tribalistic" in terms of how group-organization is generally connoted and envisioned; with this notion goes a tendency to make the tribe and the tribesman the starting-point of analysis (Gluckman, 1961, p. 69). Tribalism has now become the primary means through which the African political leadership is conducted and a powerful tool for political mass mobilization (Paglia, 2014). This is yet another instance of class formation among Africans, as has been illustrated by tribes such as the Baganda of Uganda, the Kikuyu of Kenya, and the Ibo of Nigeria. These are just a glimpse of the scenario. It is evident that that the former colonial masters in Africa skillfully surrendered political power while maintaining economic control. Africa therefore became politically independent while still being economically in bondage (Deng, 1998, p. 8).

Shortsightedness

Current trends show that Africa still struggles with food insecurity as a recurring challenge. African nations have fertile soil; and in spite of the global warming trends that make the climate unreliable, still many African leaders have been shortsighted in this regard. It would make more sense for African leaders to invest in agriculture to improve food security. The spending on military and armaments has been unprecedented in African politics for over four decades, creating a sort of African arms race. Uganda's expenditure on arms was more than double that of Kenya's in 2011, with a new global arms expert report showing that Uganda spent US$1.02 billion (United Nations Development Programme, 2013). This amount would have been adequate to upgrade all the research hospitals in the EAC, and supply all the schools with resources needed in Uganda and Burundi for a decade.

Poor Vision (Administration and Leadership)

African administrative and leadership problems are as complex as they are multifaceted. Their resolution ultimately depends on the capacity of people who understand what kinds of leaders they should elect into office and what is happening around them, at all levels from the village chiefs to national prime ministers or presidents. The populace must possess an enhanced ability to be able to take appropriate steps towards electing leaders with great moral standards and economic discipline as well as inclusiveness that addresses the Pan-African ideology. But especially at the higher levels of leadership, Africa can take a leaf out of the books of other nations (Damiba, 1998, p. 2). Africans have been governed by a set of ideologies including proverbs. For example the proverb of the people of Lesotho, "A chief is a chief by the people" exemplifies the principles the people can apply in electing chiefs. The same principle should apply in electing the heads of states. Thus all the people of the nation come to agreement, not one tribe. As Damiba notes:

> "Unlike other parts of the world, Africa at present has no high-level think tank, no institute or a centre that engages in long-range studies, policy formulation and analysis. As a first step, therefore, the Forum should initiate action and extend assistance and collaborative efforts towards creating an African Centre or Institute for Policy and Strategic Studies." (Damiba, 1998, p. 2)

Poverty

It is not disputable that Africa is the poorest continent in the world (Ebegbulem, 2012, p. 221). The food and nutrition situation in Africa calls for immediate new and practical policy initiatives. Some of the issues African leaders would engage in would include setting up farms at various agro-ecological locations concentrating on a few major crops: staples, roots/tubers, fruits/vegetables, medicinal plants, animals and cash crops. On average, less than 60 percent of African adults can read and write with understanding. Despite improvements in universal primary education enrollments, countries in Africa still face numerous education challenges. There are a number of reasons why educational levels are low; for instance, Africa has many under-15s and thus, governments are therefore faced with the challenge of educating increasing numbers of school-aged children within tightly constrained budgets. In poorer households, education is not a priority since the families are preoccupied with searching for food and shelter for survival. In such situations, child labor is rife and children are kept out of school to work; in cases of extreme poverty, children may contribute up to 40 percent of family income. These and other constraints mean families cannot afford, or do not prioritize schooling. Thus, poverty is exacerbated by the dependency on foreign aid as illustrated in the Data Table.

Data Table			
Africa's Aid-Dependency Foreign Aid Contributes Heavily to Various Economic Indicators in Numerous Nations			
Selected Country	**GNI** (Gross National Income)	**Capital Formation**	**Imports**
Ethiopia	23	108	48
Ghana	15	55	24
Mauritania	11	55	...
Mozambique	21	101	45
Sierra Leone	34	211	87
Tanzania	16	84	53
Uganda	17	75	49
Note: Above figures in millions of USD. Source: World Bank, 2006, database; data cited in Killick and Foster (2006).			

Inept Conflict Resolution Strategies

A pervasive atmosphere of domestic unrest, tensions, and conflicts have been the greatest political challenge to Africa. The conflicts, which have often led to civil wars, have always resulted from border problems or the activities of dissidents or rebel groups across the colonial boundaries. Modern African leaders have ignored their fundamental obligation to resolve conflicts peacefully.

A chronic state of instability resulting from these internal and regional tensions and conflicts has increasingly marginalized Africa's position in the geopolitical dynamics of the global scene. This marginalization has made African states be labeled as "Failed States." Revisiting her own proverbs, Africa can make use of the proverb from the people of Lesotho which states that "a bull gets over-powered by a multitude," emphasizing the importance of unity.

Weak States and Economic Institutions

African nations are considered to be weak in economic institutions. This condition has led to the dilemma of weak states. African national boundaries are largely a result of colonial heritage, laid down with little regard for the identities of local residents. This history has resulted in countries that are marked by ethnic and religious diversity, which has been transformed into ethnic and religious conflict at the local or national level by unscrupulous politicians, resource constraints, and discrimination (Handley et al., 2009). Politics is not all that matters. This dilemma is further reinforced by systemic dysfunctions that may not be the consequence of any strategic design or the outcome of elite preferences; they might be termed "dysfunctions by default." This is why it is important to harness the musical heritage so that these peoples can share their cultural arts and help promote cohesion among them and thereby reduce conflicts. The Rwandan genocide of 1994 makes a good point of departure. Other areas with similar conflicts include South Sudan, Democratic Republic of Congo, Darfur, and northern Nigeria. In many countries, large territories are outside the control of the central government, and warlords rule through force of arms, which they often acquire by selling "blood" resources such as diamonds and timber. This is the case today in the Democratic Republic of the Congo, and during the previous decade in several West African countries. In other words, the process of nation-building is incomplete in many African states. Moreover, legal-rational state institutions are weak in countries where they compete with vibrant informal institutions or where they are deliberately emasculated to serve a political or economic agenda (Medard, 1982, pp.162–192). There are in fact few political or economic incentives for the elites to relinquish control to formal state structures and institutions, and this in turn stalls economic development.

Throwing Off the Chains

Aesthetics and Technology

The dismal state of Africa and the overall condition of its children globally are direct testaments to our "paying the price" for Black involvement in the slave trade, corrupt leadership, and horrendous mismanagement of resources. But today, despite the past, African people have a moral obligation to work diligently at throwing off the mental chains of White supremacy that paralyze Africa and keep its offspring from unleashing their optimal potential amongst the family of humanity. Modern technology intertwined with culture can be used to reposition and optimize the Continent's leverage in the 21st century; additionally, amongst itself and the general populus, national leadership should encourage resourcefulness, integrity, innovation, and management acumen as complements to cultural appreciation in fostering societal progress. As all progressive societies and peoples do, culture, associated outlook and applications are modernized and updated, thus retaining the good aspects from past eras and discarding outdated/unproductive beliefs and concepts. The transition of the Norse lands, home to the Vikings—legendary, seafaring marauders—into modern, Scandinavian nations like Finland and Norway—considered to be peaceful, industrial democracies, and experts in high-tech cruise ship-building and other constructive fields—offer instructive examples.

The visual aesthetic of traditional culture can and should be incorporated into the framework of modern African sculptures, carvings, textiles and architecture. Of particular note, fractal geometry, with its repetition of similar patterns at ever-diminishing scales, and featured in such traditional crafts/art as the Agaseke baskets made in Rwanda and Burundi, gives shape to myriad forms of human expression in African culture (Moraga, 2011, p. 119); for instance, much of African woven/textile art, such as Kente, Kitenge or Kuba, symbolically conveys proverbs, moral/spiritual precepts and/or other aspects of philosophy. The notion among some that *"modern* (technologically advanced) = Caucasian" and *"primitive* (technologically retarded) = African" should be eradicated. Modernization has no racial or ethnic overtone, but is a concept that is applicable to any culture. Technological improvements, uses and applications are not race-specific; such developments can be used by all humans for progress, and to think otherwise is conceptually errant.

Kenyan post-colonial literature theorist Ngugi wa Thiong'o notes in his novel *The River Between* that Africans who saw themselves as more Western believe that the geometry of *misonge* (circular houses in KiSwahili), an indigenous concept, is primitive in comparison to rectangular designs which they associate with Europeans (Zaslavsky, 1999, pp. 161–162). Perhaps the Black Diaspora in working with Africa and helping to optimize its potential may do so in part out of cultural ties, common ancestry and pride, but also because of an inner desire to return some day or regularly visit a well-kept ancestral home. The Black Diaspora is Africa in the far corners of its soul, for it is only a collective representation of peoples removed from Africa by time and distance. Black people should rediscover their African selves and use/engage their ancient homeland and a reconnection to it as a resource for themselves; these initiatives are part of the process of healing the scars and cultural memory of racism and associated abuse. Additionally, the incorporation of African business, culture and technology news programming (e.g., *CNBC Africa*, *Bloomberg TV Africa*, *VOA's TV2 Africa* and *The Africa Channel*), as part of mainstream cable TV packages across the US, Canada and Europe, will be useful in generating Diaspora interest and involvement in Africa as a multilevel resource. Petition efforts and campaigns to facilitate this corporate move should be vigorously pursued.

Africa's resources and the ingenuity of its children permeate the fabric of US society in numerous areas; for example:

- **language terms/lexicon**—jumbo, safari
- **crafts**—handcrafted Gullah sweetgrass baskets made and sold across South Carolina and Georgia, or Rwandan Agaseke baskets sold as Macy's items
- **food/cooking**—yams, fritters, gumbo, coffee, rice cultivation, babbake (bah-bah-kay; Hausa source word for the concept and practice of barbecue or barbecuing) (Twitty, 2015)
- **music**—conga drum, marimba, jazz, kalimba, ivory piano keys
- **agro-industrial development**—African slave labor was the engine behind early US agricultural and industrial fortunes.
- **Black generated-sports revenue**—The NFL, NBA and NCAA generate megabucks and provide lucrative jobs for sports analysts, accountants and other associated professionals as a large consequence of Black athletic talent. Advertisers pay an average of US$4.5million per 30 seconds of commercial airtime during the Super Bowl. ESPN, as the host network, invested US$7.3billion in the inaugural 2014–15 College Football Playoff.
- **technology**—mpingo, the primary wood for clarinets and oboes; neodymium, a mainly Namibian rare earth element used to make the motor magnets in hybrid/electric cars;

coltan, a mainly Congo mineral used to optimize energy storage via capacitors in electronic devices like cell phones and laptops

In this light, since life and culture in the land of their birth has been shaped and molded in part by Black hands, African Americans have a duty and responsibility to showcase, cultivate and visibly articulate their heritage, Africa's presence and essence, in the US and to the world, for example by wearing of African or African-inspired clothes as part of professional dress at work, church, and/or business confabs; legal adoption of traditional/indigenous African names; giving African names to institutions, organizations and initiatives; and promotion of research, seminars and information to facilitate and encourage the use, discovery and mass awareness of Africanisms that exist in the Americas (Katembo, B., 2012, pp. 9–10).

African Americans should insist upon and advocate for their cultural equality to be a pillar of a multicultural, multiracial modern US—a virtual country of nations, a geopolitical space where different races and ethnicities share a home with others. Essentially, they can use and acknowledge Africa as a present-tense resource for themselves and for the soil on which they reside. Branches are an important part of a tree; in parallel, peoples of the African continent and its Diaspora are a key resource whose energies can be interfaced and robustly channeled toward rebuilding their ancestral soul and home, Africa.

Introspection and Cultural Exploration

In the US particularly, Blacks have been historically under constant siege ranging from physical brutality to socio-economic marginalization and discrimination across all aspects of society. Even though significant social progress and civil rights gains like voting and public accommodations have been made over the last half-century through the removal of apartheid laws and numerous efforts to promote multicultural inclusion and democracy, Blacks still face widespread subtle, and not so subtle, racial discrimination and inequities in housing, employment, education, capital access via loans and grants, and the judicial system. Long-term disenfranchisement affects the behavior, perspectives, and outlook of the victimized. For large numbers of Black citizens, socio-economic marginalization and a poor quality of life overall—extensions of the effects of slavery, apartheid, and other forms of systemic racism—are a fact ... a seemingly ongoing punishment of varying degrees; in essence, citizenship has not been complete despite noted progress.

The chronic lingering of these conditions hardens perceptions that Blacks are a downtrodden people who are unable to craft and pursue options and strategies which will curtail group abuse. Civil rights can be defined as the liberties and privileges granted by a country to a citizen of the associated nation. The Civil Rights Movement of the 1950s–1960s, orchestrated by African people in the US, sought full citizenship—voting rights, access to public accommodations, equal protection under the law—within what could be construed as a White-controlled, racist, apartheid-oriented society at the time. It epitomized a justifiable quest for full citizenship, full participation and full inclusion by Black people in a country which their slave ancestors contributed significantly to building. The basic goals of that movement have been achieved, though constant vigilance and monitoring to preserve/maintain those rights are prudent and needed. Civil rights do not ensure acceptance, equality and progress in a given society for any people, particularly Black people in this case under discussion; it merely provides a legal conduit for societal movement, acknowledgement of basic rights, and constitutional redress of grievances.

Though civil rights are needed for any people to live in a society, its quest in the US for Black people has largely spoken to an image and vibe of victimization; hence, in metaphorical terms, it can give mental imagery to the White supremacy adage, the *pitiful and downtrodden Negro … a most unfortunate race.* The African American population, like any other group living in the US, must find its own customized and functional way to circumvent prejudices and develop niches as an advancement pathway. The focus now should be human rights; that is, unearned privileges inherited simply by being a person. To secure these rights requires an ongoing activation, articulation and application of the seven (7) major elements of culture: *social organization* (views of society, family and "right and wrong"); *history* (a chronicling of past events), inclusive of customs and traditions; *mythology* (a people's set of beliefs or stories), inclusive of religion, folktales, fables and secular/sacred assumptions; *ethos* (character of a people and their distinctive achievements); *economic organization* (use of resources and ideas/strategies regarding business/commerce); *political organization* (social capacity and leverage); and *creative motif* (aesthetic), inclusive of language, art, music, literature and technology. Human rights encompass much more than civil rights; in fact, civil rights collectively are a component of human rights. Malcolm X, slain nationalistic theorist and human rights advocate, said that citizenship is a by-product of human rights recognition which means (in context to the United States) that if the human rights of Black people were really respected throughout the society, civil rights abuses like voter suppression tactics, racial profiling and police brutality would be negligible. Unlike civil rights, human rights are not based upon needing permission or consent from others. The declaration of human rights is an act of *kujichagulia* (self-determination); this is powerful because your destiny is in your own hands, not in the control of others. As humans, we have natural rights (AKA human rights) which trump those granted by a political state; these must be optimized for any distinct people to be whole, productive and in keeping with how the Creator intended.

With the actualization of human rights, these described, aforementioned circumstances of siege, discrimination, and oppression can be remedied if group efforts were commenced to utilize Africa as a leverage tool and resource. As peoples who were stolen/forcibly removed from Africa via the slave trade (with Africans colluding with Caucasians (and Asians (Indians) to some degree) and figuring prominently in the *capturer-and-supplier* component role) and then brutally exploited as slave laborers to build the Americas' colonial (European) economies or as tusk donkeys to haul ivory hundreds of miles for Arab and Indian business interests, African Americans and other Diaspora Africans have earned the right to simultaneously reside, communicate and participate in political and economic affairs between the lands of their birth and current citizenship and those of their African ancestry; thus, the Diaspora never forfeited being African nor its right (or rightful heritage) to fully participate in that ancestry and in the development of the associated nations. There are numerous ways that the contemporary African American community, the most technologically and economically potent branch of the Diaspora, may heal itself from the shackles of mental colonialism, participate in Africa's development as a resource and in turn enhance its political and economic leverage within the US; this repair and progress should include two thrusts: introspection and cultural exploration. In terms of prudence, time efficiency, and energy focus, Black people probably need to engage in self-empowerment strategies that are not centered around the coercing of Whites to redistribute wealth; basically (as a primary aim), develop and implement empowerment solutions and strategies which minimize (or do not require) White input. First, Blacks don't have the leverage and associated organizational structure at the current time to force such action, so the efforts result in futility and frustration. Second, there is seemingly no collective consciousness amongst Whites that Blacks are owed for the sins of past enslavement and the associated lingering effects and conditions. Because Black people have been unable to develop effective and doable group solutions in nullifying the parameters of White supremacy (both psychological and structural), despair, economic marginalization, high crime, *thug life* behavior and a host of other social ills have become entrenched fixtures in many African American communities.

Regarding introspection, the Black community needs to work hard to change its image, both internal and external; its views and values; and its behavior in areas of deficit and/or negative perceptions. The latter includes crime-ridden neighborhoods, low-performing public schools, slack work ethic, criminal tendencies, low character, and violent behavior especially among males. Self-improvement is the culmination of a desire to be better and to do better. In terms of collective African American cultural emphasis and cognizance, serious attention has to be devoted to appearance, dress, speech, behavior, and personal/civic responsibility. Cornerstone community emphasis must be placed on appreciation of African heritage, law-abidingness, courtesy, integrity, and other qualities of high character in order to facilitate cultural repair. The negative elements in the Black community, those characterized by the thug culture label, are unfairly used as an ethos projection for the entire race; hence, being a model citizen is seen as an exception to the rule. As a psychological tactic and tool, image makeover has aims and benefits: 1) to facilitate civility and conflict resolution amongst Black people; 2) to disarm and reduce heightened White aggression against Blacks, particularly in reference to public opinion, policing and law enforcement, and armed White citizens; 3) to increase confidence within Black circles that African American communities and activities are worthy of residence, resource investment and/or participation; and 4) to minimize negative media assault and portrayal. It should not be viewed as a manifestation of weakness or a surrendering of dignity, but merely as a survival and protection tool.

The dominant White culture collectively stereotypes Blacks as a group instead of assessing based on individual action; also, in White-controlled employment sectors, African Americans are required to exhibit greater competence than Whites to get hired or attain job advancement—recalling an old expression, "You have to be twice as good." All groups should strive to exhibit and encourage model citizenship as a matter of principle; but African Americans must be especially mindful of this aspiration, given the intensity of anti-Black societal bias and resentment. Such assertions seem unfair and are a double standard; however, they are pragmatic responses to current/existing conditions and to the *cards that have been dealt*. In reality, Blacks are a fraction of the US population (perhaps about 3/20 or 15 percent as a conservative estimate), so there are associated, inherent disadvantages and power differentials in not being the majority, particularly in legal justice, physical defense and economic prowess. Not proactively getting a handle on reducing severe negative stereotypical perceptions and media projections such as being prone to welfare dependence, freeloading, theft, and violent crime can potentially agitate a genocidal climate against African Americans, particularly Black males. Signs of this morphing siege manifest in the fact that the Black male quickly becomes the *poster child* for home invasion, rape, animal cruelty, domestic abuse, and a host of other social ills, as White tolerance and support grows for more "get tough on crime" legislation, expanded "Stand Your Ground" laws, resource divestment from public schools, racial profiling and "Whitopias" (author Rich Benjamin's coined term for purposefully emergent, 21st-century Caucasian towns, cities and communities in the US) — all of which underscore an open fear, rebuff, and dislike of Blacks. Perceptions and media portrayals about supposed Black dysfunctions (e.g., high crime rates; dismal academic achievement levels) and complaints/grievances (e.g., employment discrimination; an unfair criminal justice system) tend to galvanize and intensify existing White anger toward African Americans.

Seething escalation and potential violent consequences of this anger may not be as far beneath the surface of the social landscape as some may believe, but merely in remission until the right urge, circumstance, or release-catalyst occurs. The 1994 Hutu slaughter of Tutsis in the Rwandan Genocide, and the Nazi German massacre of Jews in the World War II era, are grim reminders of horrific genocide campaigns resulting from group demonization. As a point of emphasis, no image makeover will cure racial discrimination and hatred; however, attitudes and actions toward any specific people or community, whether sourced externally or internally, are significantly shaped by media, whether television, radio, Internet, or printed literature. Thus, every little bit helps in efforts to prevent undue backlash and to facilitate positive development, uplift, and socio-cultural parity.

The prudent and customized use of Africa as a resource is a key and often overlooked development component which will also enhance group progress in the US. Africa is a source of spiritual energy, cultural reference, and geopolitical leverage for its Diaspora—that is, a reinvestment in the collective self. There is a psychological and spiritual uplift for African Americans to see Africa positively and thus to view themselves and their heritage in a respectful light; therefore, a new consciousness eradicates the notion that their origins started on a slave ship or a plantation. New focuses will emphasize the repair of culture, the synthesis of thoughts, and the practices of a civilization. In a customized manner, identity, purpose, and direction are provided for any nation or ethnic-specific people. In addition to cultural appreciation, basic social values, which are embedded from cradle to grave, must be emphasized: be of good character; be law-abiding; have integrity; show humanity and kindness to others; develop your spiritual self, path and journey; and be a good steward of the Earth.

The second aforementioned level of repair—cultural exploration— requires activities and practical doables in the context of our current living environment. Here are some initiatives that may, upon reflection and circumstances, prove useful: investigate the use of African fabrics such as Kente for outfits or clothing accessories for varying occasions; explore and promote African history, art and artifacts, e.g., Imigongo paintings (Kabiza Wilderness Safaris Staff Writer, 2015); Ntomb'entle dolls (Mwongeli, 2015); visit African countries; share African American cultural foods and holidays such as Kwanzaa with other ethnic groups. Diaspora participation in the life of African nations is important, particularly from the perspective of shaping US–Africa trade relations, and could take the form of African American political lobby groups championing African causes before Congress. Also, an example of garnering cultural pride, dignity and respect simultaneously may be to encourage dignitaries and political candidates to wear an African textile shawl or stole, like Kente or Kuba cloth, when addressing Black organizations, paralleling in some ways the routine wearing of a yarmulke by guest speakers at Jewish confabs. Essentially, an expansion of the perspective of one's current self can come from the exploration and application of one's origin and ancestry. All of these activities will widen the perspective and cultural richness of being an African American and inevitably improve overall group leverage and self-concept; thus positive self-concept and the sharing of positive culture are conduits for bettering relations with others, in the sense of elevating what the Black community brings to the table.

The poisonous effects of slavery have encouraged the US populace, in general, to envision Africa as a place of darkness and incivility, thus contributing to a negative subconscious self-view amongst African Americans. Since the US has never respected Africa as a place of civilization, African Americans are not afforded respect in a parallel way as would Japanese Americans as extensions of Japan, a country known for high culture, industrial and economic development, and technology. The relaunch, transition and ideological transformation of Black History Month into Pan-African Heritage Month may be helpful in boosting an appreciation and positive profile of Africa. Carter G. Woodson, author of *The Mis-Education of the Negro*, created and organized Negro History Week (in 1926) as an annual, week-long February observance in segregated Black schools throughout the US. Black History Month, having gained prominence in the integration era (post-1965), is a national, month-long February commemoration in the US and Canada commemorating Black, mainly North American, contributions and achievements. It represents a relabeling and a lengthening of Negro History Week. Pan-African Heritage month, in contrast, implies a celebration of African-ness without regard to time, geography or boundaries.

Though sometimes useful, the term *Black* constitutes a racial abstract without (cultural) depth and context; conversely, *Pan-African* denotes global unity, intrinsic cultural understanding, and use of Africa as a cultural resource. *Heritage* denotes a cultural inheritance without time boundaries; history is simply a component of culture and reflects the past. In many instances and settings, Black History Month, particularly as celebrated in public schools, has been trivialized to a mentioning of redundant personalities and facts like

MLK, Rosa Parks, Malcolm X, and "Garrett Morgan invented the gas mask." An expansion and evolvement of Black History Month to Pan-African Heritage Month parallels the need to begin the application and articulation of human rights as mentioned and outlined earlier. The initial scope of Black History Month may have been pragmatic, but cannot be complete because history is only one-seventh of the cultural components. Thus, Pan-African Heritage Month celebrates the humanity of Black people in parallel with actualizing their culture and human rights. With the sheer magnitude of what Africa has done for the US, all races in the country ought to pay homage to this fact as part of a national commemoration.

Through the work of the African Diaspora in positively promoting Africa, particularly in reference to African American actions/initiatives, US citizens of all races and ethnicities are provided with a better appreciation of Africa and its contribution to the country's growth and emergence; reciprocally, respect for African Americans will grow. Diversity is a strength for the US in terms of the talent, perspectives, ideas and niche positioning of its ethnic and racial composition. African American uplift via Africa as a unique resource helps build cultural parity and helps to optimize the US's human and economic capital, and thus the strength of the country. Black cultural equality is a win-win for all.

Resource Strategies and Usage for 21st-Century Africa

Africa's stakeholders must find a way to influence the Continent's future, advocating for its best interest and safeguarding against the forces of evil intent. The empowerment and security of Africa will upgrade the economic and political leverage of all African people, whether they are in the Diaspora or on the Continent. Perhaps, the aforementioned classical definition of Pan-Africanism, largely crafted in the early 20th century, needs tweaking and expansion in application to 21ˢᵗ-century dynamics, reconceptualizing Africa as a multilevel resource amongst its Diaspora peoples. Thus, Pan-Africanism becomes operational and actualized when Africa is harnessed as a resource. There are myriads of ways in which resources are (and can be) interpreted, explained, categorized and used. For the purpose, slant and context of this work, resources (tools, possessions and assets) are branched into the categories of hard and soft. Here, *hard* is connoted as mainly dealing with minerals, plants, animals and other natural elements. *Soft* is projected and construed as dealing primarily with entities which facilitate/stimulate ideas, technology, communication, information flow and/or culture (inclusive of such physical ones like humans, laptops and/or museums).

Competition for hard resources. Africa was the target prize for European and Arab resource conquest (gold, slaves and ivory) via the respective slave trades in centuries past. The scramble for Africa's resources continues today with expanded players like the US, China, Japan and India which quest for modern resources contributing to techno-industrial maintenance, development, and growth (e.g., uranium, farmland, coltan, oil and many other products). The US and China, two titans, competitors and quasi-adversaries, seek to either maintain the status of a global superpower or emerge as one by using the acquisition of Africa's resources as a catapult. They represent two versions of capitalism (corporate-oriented and state-oriented, respectively) in their race to the top among other ferocious competitors. The scenario is reminiscent of the Old Testament story of Job in which the allegory depicts God and Satan having a conversation (and a contest/game of sorts) over Job, a good man and a mere pawn, to test and sway his loyalty to each, challenging him with a choice of allegiance; their conversation metaphorically represents a dialogue among the powerful regarding the fate and destiny of weak underlings: in the Bible, Job; in the current geopolitical context, Africa. The contest, centering on Job's endurance level of cruel afflictions induced or allowed by God or Satan, would settle their bet of superiority and one-upmanship. Ironically, according to the story Job didn't know from where or by whom these ordeals had been unleashed, from God or Satan—one good, the other evil—or maybe just two sides of the same coin. 'A Private Little War', an episode from the 1960s tv show *Star Trek*, also illustrates a struggle between powerful adversaries in which a pawn (primitive villagers, in this case) is caught in the middle. In this tale, the crew of the starship *Enterprise* discovers Klingon interference in the development of Neural, a formerly peaceful planet that is virtually a medical treasure trove of materials needed to manufacture various serums and drugs. For various reasons (resource access, influence, and perhaps other things), officers from a visiting Klingon space vessel have armed a (warlike) ethnic group with flintlocks (17th-century firearms), an overly-advanced weapon-type in comparison to the technology pace on Neural at the time. As a result, in an attempt to restore the balance of power, James T. Kirk (*Enterprise* Captain) reluctantly and unhappily makes the call for the Enterprise's engineering department to manufacture flintlocks (100) and provide them to a pacifist-oriented ethnic group for protection/ defense purposes; this move sets the stage for a future, inevitable arms race. The Klingons, a fictional race, are characterized in the original Star Trek series as brutish, yet technologically advanced. The aforementioned episode, like numerous others, tells conflict stories of good versus evil in using the *Enterprise* (a United Federation of Planets' emissary vessel from Earth) to advance concepts of democracy and freedom while Klingons symbolize an empire of tyranny, slavery and brutality.

In real life, Africa is the pawn between these two superpowers/ adversaries (China and the United States), colluding when necessary, but each seeking to appear as an angel, while depicting the other as the devil; the contest, both geo-political and economic in nature, is a race for leverage, influence and resources on the Continent because the controller of Africa represents the world's power. US engagement in Africa mainly revolves around conflict resolution/ management efforts and security issues such as ending violence in eastern Congo, the Central African Republic, and South Sudan, and combating al-Qaeda; oil and gas, however, are currently the primary trade imports received by the US from Africa. China's interests there concentrate on the extraction of natural resources, especially from mineral-rich countries like the Democratic Republic of Congo (Kushner, 2016). More than 85 percent of China's imports from Africa consist of petroleum, copper, iron, and other raw materials needed to build the Asian giant's growing domestic infrastructure and fuel its continued economic growth (Hanauer & Morris, 2014). Vast differences in the China and US trade figures with Africa also underscore the countries' divergent priorities. China–Africa trade volumes hit US$198.5 billion in 2012; by comparison, US–Africa trade in the same year was half that, reaching roughly US$100 billion. The US has made robust strides in 2014 to up its economic game in Africa, showcased by US President Barack Obama's two signature Africa initiatives: *Power Africa*, a US$7 billion project which aims to improve electric generation in African nations, and *Trade Africa*, an effort to increase US exports to the five EAC member states by 40 percent (Hanauer & Morris, 2014).

China's two-way trade with Africa has grown by 30 percent annually over the last decade; thus, in 2014, it is now Africa's largest trading partner, importing largely natural resources. Some of China's financial and infrastructure interests in Africa seem beneficial, and even necessary, if African nations themselves have a well-crafted strategic plan for using these acquisitions; for example, transport infrastructure (airports, railways, roads, and bridges, etc.), university buildings, and hospitals, just to name a few (Aljazeera Staff Writer, 2014; Smith, 2012); even the US's peacekeeping and security-oriented involvement have merit. However, no matter whether nations come to aid or trade, the resulting interactions must position Africa's nations to be on the pathway to jump-start their economies, create Africa-based industries (capable of providing jobs and producing finished-product goods), improve quality of life for the populace, engage in scientific resource management, and organize cities and territories around the optimal use of clean/renewable energy sources.

African nations should reprioritize and focus upon trade efforts with nations that offer self-sufficiency technologies in vital areas like water management, food security and renewable fuels as exchangeables for replenishable African exports. The use of self-sufficiency technologies like renewable energy and advanced irrigation techniques facilitate reduction of fossil fuels and boost food productivity from indigenous sources. Basically, non-replenishable raw materials like gold, diamonds and other hard/precious minerals need to stay in the ground as much as possible to serve as long-term economic cushion assets; once these minerals are drained and depleted, there is no replacement. In this regard, increased trade efforts with nations like the Scandinavian countries, Germany and Israel, along the lines/parameters that have been mentioned, may prove prudent; African nations can lessen food imports, strengthen food security capabilities, and minimize food shortages due to drought by prioritizing significant use of resource management techniques and renewable energy as imperative initiatives.

The Scandinavian countries and Germany are the most ardent and visible proponents of clean and green technologies. Germany's energy supply from green sources is at the 25 percent level according to 2013 figures; the country has a goal of 35 percent green energy reliance by 2020 (Charig, 2012). Norway aims to have 67.5 percent of its energy consumption from renewable sources by 2020 (Holter, 2013). The country is a pioneer in renewable energy and environmental technology, with hydro and wind as research emphases and solar as an increasing interest; nearly all the electric energy generated there derives from hydroelectric power (Invest in Norway, 2014), given its vast water resources.

In contrast, Israel, a small country with a dry/arid climate and 60 percent sand coverage and a nation positioned in a desert ecosystem, is a food exporter and the leading source of effective irrigation across the globe (e.g., for production of desert-grown tomatoes and peaches); additionally, this desert nation has made notable strides and innovations in resource management, particularly fish farming and water technology (desalinization, drip irrigation), agro-genetic engineering (genetically modified seeds), dry-land agriculture, and usage of multiple water types (salty, recycled, rain, brackish, fresh, bilge) (Blum, 2014; Schuster, 1999). Israel's signature water technology innovation is drip irrigation, which saves/conserves water and fertilizer by allowing water to drip slowly to the roots of plants through a network of valves, pipes, tubing and emitters (East Africa Agribusiness Staff Writer, 2014; Sales, 2014); it basically facilitates use of minimal water to produce optimum crop yield. Starting in the early 2000s, Israeli farmers have used 30 percent less water while doubling crop output, leaving the country with a 150 percent food surplus (Reuters Staff Writer, 2010). Israel's resource management expertise, particularly as related to water technology and desert-farming know-how, is vital to Africa's arid growing regions, which risk becoming increasingly vulnerable to climate change.

Collectively, Africa's diverse soils, topography, climatic conditions, and natural resources (like waterways, wind and abundant sunlight) make it an ideal place where all the aforementioned technologies can be strategically harnessed for optimum crop and energy production. Besides raw minerals, Africa, with aggressive cultivation, has much to offer others in trade, commerce and resources, tourism; and new innovations in the use of renewable energy. However, fresh paradigms must be envisioned and actualized in order to design, advance and promote new resources and rethink how old ones can be properly managed. Africa's indigenous biofuel infrastructure and production can be ramped up, via commercial farming and refinement, to sell oil derived from plants like Jatropha as biodiesel fuel to countries such as Israel, Germany and Norway in exchange for technical assistance. As with the nature of trade, there is a two-way flow of exchange goods; therefore African nations must envision what resources can be provided to the trading partner, emphasizing abundant replenishable goods.

As one practical step, a proposed relationship between Israel and South Sudan (the world's newest nation) can be examined. South Sudan, a nation with a dry/arid climate and unpredictable rainfall, exclusively depends on oil sales for budget funding and revenue; development of other resource sectors such as eco- and conference tourism could lessen this dependence. Other major resources include timber, abundant sunlight, gold, diamonds, and part of the Nile River as a topographical feature (Farhat, 2012; Guardian Staff Writer, 2014); additionally, the country has large, uncultivated regions containing significant quantities of elephants, giraffe, buffalo, gazelle, hippos, and rare birds like shoebills—an ideal resource for developing a game park tourism industry (Wildlife Conservation Society Writer, 2013). To be properly launched, this potential industry needs logistical planning (conservation/land-use analysis), vision, and funding. The Wildlife Conservation Society (WCS) identifies the 200,000-square-kilometer Boma–Jonglei landscape in South Sudan as the largest, substantially intact wildlife habitat in East Africa. In addition to animals, the region includes high-altitude plateaus, wooded and grassland savannas, and wetlands. Its potential is thought to rival the famed Serengeti of East Africa (Rucker, 2011). South Sudan can provide Israel with access to specified quantities of Nile water (a current negotiation effort), limited timber, and allowance of joint Israel–South Sudanese security-force cooperation in protecting South Sudan's borders and interior from potential infestations by anti-Israeli/anti-Jewish terrorist groups like al-Qaeda and al-Shabaab. In exchange, Israel can provide South Sudan with technology expertise for water or clean energy, particularly solar, and security-force assistance including training, advisors, and surveillance technology for repelling ivory poachers, the Lord's Resistance Army, Boko Haram and other aforementioned terrorist entities. Such assistance would be vital respectively to food production, clean water access and electrical power, and the emergence/maintenance of a positive business climate. In a peaceful and safe environment, eco- and conference tourism can flourish and develop; tourism and the complementary hospitality and retail industries will facilitate and generate employment opportunities and revenue dollars for the local economy. The outlined Israel–South Sudan trade scenario can be a core model for how African nations engage the globe with respect to commerce; that is, with acquisition of self-sufficiency technologies and primary emphasis on exporting replenishable goods.

Soft resource strategies. In complement to and synthesis with hard resources such as natural assets (e.g., minerals; wood; water), many of Africa's strengths lay in the development and cultivation of soft resources like innovation, tourism, literature, architecture, ideas, crafts and cultural arts such as music. For example, African farmers can engage in stimulating agricultural innovation systems that can enhance Africa's food security and capacity building. In the health sector, the current population of African researchers is ageing such that young, talented researchers are needed as replacements (Whitworth et al., 2008). Many young Africans have the human capacity to engage in health-oriented education if given that opportunity through African internal educational collaboration supported by joint global stake holders in education such the Bill and Melinda Gates Foundation. The inherent innovative capacity of the young African can also be seen in the work of contemporary scientists such as Dr. Victor Ogungbe, a Nigerian microbiology professor at Jackson State University, whose research is geared towards preclinical drug discovery, particularly in the development effort of a new drug to fight and attack *Plasmodium*, a malaria-causing parasite.

Until quite recently, the Western world accorded no place in its architectural schema regarding Africa, except in reference to Egypt (Prussin, 1974). As a matter of fact, equally attractive in the modern day architectural designs are African artifacts which can be harnessed to influence global architectural designs. In the book *Revealing the African Presence in Renaissance Europe* (Spicer et al., 2012), the varied roles and societal contributions of African descendents in Renaissance Europe are depicted in compelling paintings, drawings, sculpture, and printed books of the period. This research is a clear indication that if Africans established centers that would archive these artifacts, global tourists would tap into these by not only visiting Africa frequently and contributing to Africa's tourism industry, but also by engaging in direct trade with the African curators.

Finally, music, another important African soft resource, is the vortex of religious ritual. It traditionally provided an avenue for musicians to naturally engage in artistic creations throughout their livelihood. The problem with these activities is that they were hardly ever harnessed as an economy-generation endeavor. In Africa, people generally engage in their cultural musical activities with group roles through vocal music. In addition to these roles, Africans also perform these songs for entertaining themselves on musical instruments. When the community is in favor of the music, the community joins in and develops other tones to create naturally blended harmonies. Great examples can be realized in the music of *chimurenga* by Thomas Mapfumo of the Shona people of Zimbabwe, in which he mixes both European instruments and the Zimbabwean Mbira instruments to inspire both the contemporary and neo-traditional African music lovers. These songs use interesting *ostinatos* or repetitive patterns and musical timbres that are culturally aesthetic and can be used to generate economy in the music market.

While African musical instruments have a complex socio-cultural significance, they can also be used for generating economy by providing the instrument makers with an avenue to export their products. The djembe drum for example, has become a significant addition of a musical aesthetic within the instrumental music genre. In keeping with their intricate musical system, the African musicians have used every known type of portable instrument. The four categories of instruments are chordophones, idiophones, membranophones and aerophones. For this reason, it is important to examine the African society in the cultural contexts in which portable instruments can be archived in Museums of African History both in Africa and in the industrialized nations to generate income for the African musicians who make them. Establishments such as the Smithsonian Institute and Museums of Art can provide an economic base market outlet for the African instrument makers.

The use and availability of soft resources complement those of hard resources. Their tandem use optimizes the associated system of assets. Africa has an abundance of both, making the package of the Continent's assets unique. If parlayed correctly, soft resources, like hard resources, will help Africa build economic strengths, technological infrastructure, global leverage and overall economic influence.

Future of Pan-Africanism

The time has come for Pan-Africanism to evolve from ideas into practical use and development. African leaders need to embrace the African Diaspora and utilize its people as resources to enhance social and economic development both in Africa and among the Diaspora.There are many African Americans and other Diaspora Africans, particularly Canadian, EU, and Caribbean citizens, who simultaneously recognize the gamut of African regions/nations as their ancestral home and a resource; a sizeable constituency of highly educated and skilled people among this population is another asset layer and tappable resource in conjunction with a natural desire for cultural bonding. However, a workable and non-complicated plan and opportunity conduit has to be created to actualize the concepts. The collective African Diaspora, coupled with Continental Africans, should be provided with the opportunity to participate in the growth, development, and life of African nations on multiple levels— economic, political, and socio-cultural. This type of networking opportunity can be referenced by emphasis on common themes and ideas which facilitate cooperation and relationship building; some identifiable anchor themes and constructs on which to build unity are: common human source region (East-Central Africa); common cultural root (Bantu); and recognition of a Pan-African language (KiSwahili). Some scientific research points to East-Central Africa as the birthplace of humanity; the specific region generally posited by researchers to contain the initial footprint of humans lies within the landscape between eastern Congo, the southern area of South Sudan, and the western areas of Uganda and Tanzania. The present-day boundaries of Africa, all of which are relatively new and artificially/arbitrarily configured, should be leapfrogged to hone in on common origin as a unity pillar.

Regarding a common cultural root, *Bantu* is a unifying ethnic/sociolinguistic term for people who identify themselves as being of African descent/heritage; the term mainly denotes a large family of related African languages in vocabulary and syntax, all having some form of the root word *ntu* in denoting a person, a human being (Kaula, 1968, p.1; Ochieng, 2016). *Bantu*, unlike *Negro*, emanates from indigenous Black African linguistic roots; *Negro*, on the other hand, is sourced from the Latin word *Niger* as the linguistic parent. Latin contains three gender-based adjectives meaning dark or Black: *nigra* (feminine); *niger* (masculine); *nigrum* (neuter); these root words have spawned numerous noun variations denoting an African, a field worker or servitude in the Romance languages—*negro* (Spanish; Portuguese), *negre* (French)—and in the Germanic languages—*negar/neggar* (Dutch), *neger/negger* (German), *nigger* (US English). Even in the Bible (NIV), Simeon, mentioned as one of the teachers and prophets in the church of Antioch, was called Niger in Acts 13:1; that is, Simeon Niger (or Simeon the Niger in other text versions), as a reference to dark skin and presumed African descent. Several centuries ago, White social scientists like German anthropologist Johann Friedrich Blumenbach (1752–1840) popularized *Negro* as the accepted scientific literature/journal term for Black people, the African race. Prior to the 21st century, Negroid, Caucasoid and Mongoloid were the adjectives routinely used to respectively identify and group humanity into the contemporary racial categories of Africans, Caucasians and Asians. The selection of Niger and Nigeria as names for African countries is indicative of colonial domination and long-held, accepted views about racial classification; in contrast, indigenous names facilitate internal power to shape self-definition and perception.

Many negative connotations like laziness and stupidity have been made synonymous with the term Negro. These attributes paralleled the position of servitude occupied by Blacks in Africa and in the Diaspora during the periods of slavery and colonialism; for example, *negrero*, a Spanish word, means tyrannical, a cruel boss, or a driver of Negroes (in the literal sense). With some progress having been made on global human rights, cultural sensitivity and efforts to eradicate racism, the use of *Negro* as the main global description of Black people has become somewhat archaic in the emergence of the 21st century. However, there does not seem to be a consensus on a linguistically indigenous African cultural term which groups Blacks globally at the same comparative level of weight and comprehensiveness as Caucasian is used to identify peoples who descend from European and/or Middle Eastern ancestries.

The term *Bantu* speaks to African humanity. As the ancestral background of most Africans, it captures the essence, ethos, and cultural heritage of Africa in a nutshell; the term is simple but accurate in defining Black people and their associated cultural ancestry irrespective of current geographies, nationalities, and languages (Saidykhan, 2010; Kenny, 2014).The proto-Bantu language is thought to have begun spreading across the African continent between 4,000 and 5,000 years ago from the Mambilla Plateau (postulated Bantu homeland located within the Nigeria-Cameroon border area) via the historic Bantu Expansion, a millennia-long series of human migrations (Omoniyi, 2013). Over time, it subdivided into many offshoots which now dominate the indigenous linguistic landscape of Africa, particularly the sub-Saharan region; some noted

Bantu languages are KiSwahili, IsiZulu, LiNgala, and KiShona, just to name a few (Biddulph, 2001). In the US, the term *Bantu* being added to the census and to race category option boxes alongside the present terms *Black* and *African American* is ancestrally valid/ comprehensive and elevates cultural dignity. Also, the name *Bakala*, a Bantu-based word meaning "people of vital energy," is discussed in the book *The BAKALA of North America* as an ethnically-specific replacement term for African American (Imhotep, 2009). Actually, the predominant African influence on African Americans emanates from Bantu culture. For example, the roots of Jazz and Gospel music are found in the Congo; yam derives from *nyami*, a Nigerian Bantu word in the Ewondo language. Actually, the first African slaves transported to Virginia (1619) were documented to have emanated from Angola, a Bantu-speaking territory (Heywood & Heywood, 2007); research shows that nearly one-fourth of the slaves imported into the US over the entire span of the Trans-Atlantic Slave Trade were shipped from Angola (Gates, Jr. & Amos, 2013).

All races can benefit from using an ancestrally indigenous name for group identification and classification. Eventual self-reclassification and self-reconceptualization of Black people in a global sense as Bantoid/Bantu alongside the other major racial denotings of Caucasian and Asian will underscore a mental evolution which parallels a cultural emphasis—hence, human rights. Self-definition often reflects one's view of *ubuntu* (Nguni term for "humanity," sometimes translated as "I am because of you") which underscores the often-expressed concept that "a person is a person through other people." Ubuntu, a philosophy of unity and cooperation, is about finding common ground from one human to another; it is an attitude and way of thinking (Nelson & Lundin, 2010, p.119). As a pillar, Pan-Africanist concept, its practice and emphasis amongst

African people will minimize (and eventually heal) tribalism, inter-ethnic conflict, colorism and other divisions.

Linguistically speaking, the promotion, recognition, and use of KiSwahili as an African common language is an additional, core thrust in strengthening Pan-Africanism. Former Tanzanian president Julius Nyerere, former South African president Nelson Mandela and Nigerian poet and playwright Wole Soyinka, all of whom are noted and distinguished voices from across Africa, have embraced the idea of KiSwahili as a common language. They saw the march toward unity and common understanding actualized in this effort.

As a lexiconal synthesis of at least ten Bantu languages, KiSwahili operates as the cultural common language throughout East and Central Africa with numerous speakers in West-Central and Southern Africa. It is the African continent's largest indigenous language by both geography (approximately 16 countries) and the number of speakers (about 120 million) (Katembo, B., 2012, pp. 35–36). Because of KiSwahili's unique history and positioning, ethnocentrism as an associated consequence is not evoked. The roots of it are sourced in the collective language dialects of the Mijikenda (Mee-jee-kane-dah), a Bantu people, comprised of nine (9) linguistically-linked sub-ethnicities (Giriama, Jibana, Digo, Chonyi, Kauma, Kambe, Duruma, Ribe, and Rabai). These ethnic groups are residentially-clustered

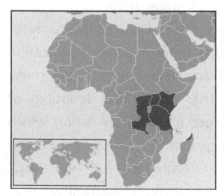

KiSwahili Epicenter Region

This map, highlighting the primary KiSwahili linguasphere (darkened areas), appears as a component of the Wikipedia entry *Swahili Language*.

along a 1000-mile East African coastal strip extending from the bottom of Somalia down to the top of Mozambique. Mijikenda is translated as 'the nine communities', with reference to the Bantu terms miji (villages) and kenda (nine); KiMijikenda is the linguistic name for the collective dialects/sub-languages of the Mijikenda. In addition to KiSwahili, there are more than 1,000 African languages that are categorized as Bantu, e.g., IsiZulu, KiKamba, LiNgala, SiSwati, etc. As mentioned earlier, they all use some form of 'ntu' to denote a person; hence, Bantu means people, given the plural prefix 'ba'. Another feature of Bantu languages is the use of the words kumi or longo (or some derivation thereof) to represent ten.

The identified countries in which KiSwahili is currently spoken in varying degrees are: Tanzania, Kenya, Burundi, Rwanda, Uganda, Central African Republic, Democratic Republic of Congo, South Sudan, Somalia, Zambia, Malawi, Mozambique, Comoro Islands, Mauritius, Seychelles, and Madagascar (allAfrica Staff Writer, 2014; Indiana University African Studies Website Team, 2014; Omondi, 2011). KiSwahili is rapidly becoming a language of business, research, and scholarship; it was also used used as a communication tool within the African/anti-colonial liberation struggles of Angola, South Africa and the US (Black Power Movement) and currently serves as one of the African Union's working languages. Thus, there is an underlying cohesion when a people have a recognized, common language ... a much-needed component for Africa and its Diaspora. As a reference example, KiSwahili is a linkage conduit between the EAC and African Americans via Kwanzaa—a KiSwahili-articulated, annual 7-day Pan-African holiday celebrated in the US. The goals and objectives of the EAC represent both a multi-ethnic meld initiative and a *harambee* (pulling together) spirit that should be emulated and customized by other African regions. EAC leaders should endeavor to establish KiSwahili as the lingua franca for the EAC. If African leaders find this plausible, they can engage themselves with the EAC policies that enhance linguistic integration for Africans in Africa and Africans in the Diaspora.

Outreach efforts are useful to facilitate networking and foster understanding; to this end, in promoting a synthesis of fun and social interaction, perhaps organizations can organize the simultaneous celebration of events in Africa and in the Diaspora; for example, the celebration of an EAC-sponsored festival, like JAMAFest, in North America (Opobo, 2013); and the coordination of Kwanzaa activities in South Africa and in various EAC sites. Another small, but significant, measure to promote connectedness is African Diaspora dual-citizenship in African nations; this provision will be a win-win situation for all parties involved: for Africa, a boost in overseas investment, tourism, and skills transfer; for the Diaspora, increased political/commerce-oriented leverage in countries of residence, and facilitation of Africa as a cultural resource conduit. From a regional perspective, the EAC is probably a great starting place from which to include interested Diasporans as a development resource and asset, for a variety of reasons. The EAC has a Pan-African flavor already in its effort to integrate multicultural African populations (In2EastAfrica, 2013); therefore, African American inclusion in the EAC as a scenario reference would simply be just another group of Africans being added to the mix. Additionally, Gabon, Namibia, Botswana, and Zambia should be included in the big picture vision of Diaspora outreach on the Continent, due to these nations' stable political structure, vast resources, good infrastructure and, in the case of Gabon and Namibia, relative proximity to the Americas.

Effective citizenship requires commitment to and knowledge of the country with which one identifies. This includes the knowledge of government, social structures, and the specific challenges the society faces. Many members of the African Diaspora have expressed a need to be granted the opportunity for dual-citizenship with the nations of Africa … an endeavor of mutual benefit for all. Inclusion of Diaspora Africans will in the long term aid the continent of Africa by enabling investment, tourism, and international resource exchange such as skills transfer and trade. As a specific point of note, African Americans will benefit tremendously by dual-citizenship with an African nation because access to US resources for Blacks is generally limited to a few sectors: education; technology exposure; basic living amenities (food, shelter and clothing); medical care; selected professional jobs like an accountant, pharmacist, plumber, public school teacher or NBA player which are all direct extensions of having specialized degrees, training, and/or skills, e.g., CPA license, Pharm.D. degree, professional educator certificate, plumbing license, etc.; thus, commercial infrastructure and most industries there are virtually already controlled and gate-kept by White people. In general, the United States, as previously mentioned, offers resources of survival to Blacks while an African nation, in addition to some basic amenities, may offer a positive outlet for culture, wide-ranging/large-scale economic opportunities (e.g., aviation industry; IT; clean energy; commercial foods), and other advantages as assets. Truthfully, residence in any nation offers triumphs and challenges, such that hurdles must be overcome with insightful navigation; the United States, an African nation or any other country are no exception to this reality. Since a package of resources may not always be found in the same space or area, multi-residence facilitates comprehensive, amalgamated resource access with which to create individual wealth or group leverage; in the case of African Americans, the benefits of dual-citizenship, i.e., simultaneously having a homeland and a new home, outweigh the negatives. In this arrangement, Diaspora Africans and their descendants gain additional and expanded access to lucrative employment, business venture opportunities, a vacation (and/or retirement) destination, a heritage/cultural link and most importantly, a summative investment in 'self.' Because of the subtle (and not so subtle) aspects/constructs of White supremacy in the US, Blacks there, for survival, have to expend too much time and energy thinking about White people and racism and how to confront and navigate around both. For African Americans particularly, multi-residence can also foster health and psycho-social benefits: a respite and stress relief from emotional depression, energy-drain and racism (real or perceived) in an atmosphere which forces activism and constant vigilance in response to racial discrimination and White-privilege; an opportunity to engage in a potentially exciting, uplifting environment; a conduit to cultivate new ideas, tension reduction, and a catharsis or mental rejuvenation, so that ongoing interracial relationships in the US, especially with White people, can take on a more amicable, non-confrontational tone and an equitable dynamic. Significant measures to facilitate such an effort are greatly needed.

Several African economic blocs, such as ECOWAS (Economic Community of West African States) and SADC (Southern African Development Community), have been developed in the past five decades; unfortunately, they have not met the expectations of the Diaspora in terms of outreach, resource optimization, development goals and other issues of concern. However, the EAC, a regional intergovernmental organization based in Arusha, Tanzania, is an interesting case in point regarding a bloc with great potential; it oversees and facilitates the cultural, economic and eventual political integration of the confederated, multicultural region comprised of Kenya, Uganda, Tanzania, Rwanda, Burundi, and soon-to-be South Sudan. Its leaders should expand the opportunity of inclusion, via dual-citizenship or multilevel participation, to include interested African Americans and Africans living in other Diaspora locations.

Relationships take time to cultivate and also come with challenges. Building them is a process and has to be anchored on strong foundations for success. The Pan-African Factor (or Pan-Africanism), as an extension of networking, cooperation and building relationships, is a conduit for endless benefits and greater heights in African development. Planning and strategy are paramount to linking the talents, skills and resources of Continental and Diasporan Africans in facilitating Africa's rebirth. This evolution will be facilitated by new thinking, new paradigm conceptualizations, new African-oriented educational content models and an emphasis on similarities as opposed to differences amongst African peoples, a truly global race.

Bibliography

Abraham, J. (2014, April 25). *Zambia's roaring tourism industry.* [Video file]. Retrieved from https://www.youtube.com/watch?v=udvMeonVSBI

Abrams, S. (2016). Your blackness isn't like mine: Colorism and oppression olympics. *The Huffington Post.* Retrieved from http://www.huffingtonpost.com/sil-lai-abrams/your-blackness-isnt-like-_b_10704520.html

Acemoglu, D. & Robinson, J. (2004). Institutions as a fundamental cause of long-run growth. *National Bureau of Economic Research, NBER Working Paper No. 10481.*

Adams, D. (2007). Sweetgrass baskets. *Beaufort County Library.* Retrieved from http://www.beaufortcountylibrary.org/htdocs-sirsi/sweetgra.htm

Aharone, E.(2003). *Pawned sovereignty: Sharpened Black perspectives on Americanization, Africa, war and reparations.* Bloomington, IN: AuthorHouse.

Ahmed, B. (2016). 'We are being hunted like animals:' Malawi's albino people are threatened by human poachers. *THINKPROGRESS.* Retrieved from http://thinkprogress.org/world/2016/03/04/3756677/malawi-albino/

Akombo, D. O. (2006). *Music and healing across cultures*. Ames, IA: Culicidae Press.

Akoto, K. A. (1992). *Nationbuilding: Theory and practice in African centered education*. Washington, DC: African World Institute.

Akoto, K. A., & Akoto, A. N. (1999).*The Sankofa movement*. Washington, DC: OyokoInfoCom.

Akwagyiram, A. (2013). Portugal's unemployed heading to Mozambique 'paradise'. *BBC News*. Retrieved from http://www. bbc.com/news/world-africa-22025864

Algemeiner Staff Writer. (2012). The rise of Israeli fish farming. *The Algemeiner*. Retrieved from http://www.algemeiner. com/2012/09/07/the-rise-of-israeli-fish-farming/

Aljazeera Staff Writer. (2014). China to build railway linking East Africa. *Aljazeera*. Retrieved from http://www.aljazeera. com/news/africa/2014/05/china-build-railway-linking-east-africa-201451263352242135.html

Aljazeera Staff Writer. (2016). Africa's big men: The continent's long-serving leaders. *Aljazeera*. Retrieved from http://www. aljazeera.com/indepth/interactive/2016/04/africa-big-men-continent-long-serving-leaders-160424144247278.html

Aljazeera Staff Writer. (2016). Burundi violence: Africa 'will not allow genocide.' *Aljazeera*. Retrieved from http://www. aljazeera.com/news/2015/12/burundi-deploy-experts-monitor-violence-151217142631031.html allAfrica Staff Writer. (2014). Tanzania: Congo invites Kiswahili teachers. *allAfrica*. Retrieved from http://allafrica.com/stories/201408150861.html

Allen, S. (2015). Georgetown's new court will feature Allen Iverson era Kente-cloth pattern. *The Washington Post*. Retrieved from https://www.washingtonpost.com/news/dc-sports-bog/wp/2015/06/09/georgetowns-new-court-will-feature-allen-iverson-era-kente-cloth-pattern/

Alpers, E. (1967). *The east African slave trade*. [Published as paper no. 3 for the Historical Association of Tanzania]. Nairobi, Kenya: East African Publishing House.

Anderson, B. (2016). Black state lawmaker says declaration of independence is racist. *DOWNTREND.com*. Retrieved from http://downtrend.com/71superb/black-state-lawmaker-says-declaration-of-independence-is-racist

Anwisye, S. (2009). The African personality: Lubrication for liberation. St. Louis, MO: AFDJ.

Aochamub, A. (2009). Boldly branding Namibia. *The Namibian*. Retrieved from http://www.namibian.com.na/index.php?id=35357&page=archive-read

Appiah, K. (1999). Ethnicity and identity in Africa: An interpretation. In *Africana: The encyclopedia of the African and African-American experience* (p. 703). New York, NY: Civitas Books.

Arensen, J. (1983). *Sticks & straw: Comparative house forms in southern Sudan and northern Kenya*. Dallas, TX: International Museum of Cultures.

Asante, M. K. (1998). *The Afrocentric idea*. Philadelphia, PA: Temple University Press

Asante, M. K. (2000). *The Egyptian philosophers: Ancient African voices from Imhotep to Akhenaten*. Chicago, IL: African American Images.

ATA. (2015, September 30). *ATA's 10th annual presidential forum on tourism*. [Video file]. Retrieved from https://www.youtube.com/watch?v=f83STCsjtpM

Auerbach, J. (1987). Turning sand into land. Desert farms in Israel grow lush crops from sand and salty water. *Christian Science Monitor*. Retrieved from http://www.csmonitor.com/1987/0519/dsand.html

Auty, R. M. (1998). Resource abundance and economic development: Improving the performance of resource rich countries. *Research for Action, 44*. Helsinki, Finland: WIDER.

Ayittey, G. (2016). Disband the African Union. *Foreign Policy*. Retrieved from http://foreignpolicy.com/2016/07/10/disband-the-african- union/

Ball, C. (2015). Why black America should appropriate African dress more often. *Madame Noire*. Retrieved from http://madamenoire.com/585691/black-america-should-appropriate-african-dress-more/

Ball, C. (2016). African Union says Haiti not African enough to have membership. *Madame Noire*. Retrieved from https://madamenoire.com/699128/african-union-haiti/

Barras, C. (2013). The father of all men is 340,000 years old. *New Scientist*. Retrieved from http://www.newscientist.com/article/dn23240-the-father-of-all-men-is-340000-years-old.html

BBC Reporter. (2016). Four more ways the CIA has meddled in Africa. *BBC*. Retrieved from http://www.bbc.com/news/world-africa-36303327

Benjamin, N. (1998). Trading activities of Indians in East Africa (with special reference to slavery) in the nineteenth century. *The Indian Economic and Social History Review*, 35(4), 405–420.

Benjamin, R. (2009). *Searching for Whitopia: An improbable journey to the heart of White America*. New York, NY: Hyperion.

Bever, L. (2016). Yale dishwasher resigns after smashing 'racist, very degrading' stained-glass window. *The Washington Post*. Retrieved from https://www.washingtonpost.com/news/grade-point/wp/2016/07/12/yale-dishwasher-resigns-after-smashing-racist-very-degrading-stained-glass-window/

BDlive Staff Writer (2015). Ivorians take little notice of whitening cream ban. *BDlive*. Retrieved from http://www.bdlive.co.za/africa/africannews/2015/08/11/ivorians-take-little-notice-of-whitening-cream-ban

Biddulph, J. (2001). *Bantu byways: Some explorations among the languages of Central and Southern Africa*. Cymru, Wales: Joseph Biddulph.

Birdsall, N., & Londoño, J. (1997). Asset Inequality does matter: Lessons from Latin America. *Research Department Publications*, 4066. Paris, France: Inter-American Development Bank— Research Department.

Blackstone, J. (2016). Report: Exonerated football player cites "privilege" in Stanford rape case. *CBS News*. Retrieved from http://www.cbsnews.com/news/ report-brian-banks-privilege-stanford-rape-case-brock-turner/

Blum, R. (2014). It's not the desert that's the enemy. *ISRAEL21c*. Retrieved from http://israel21c.org/environment/ its-not-the-desert-thats-the-enemy/

Bokrezion, H. (2016). Nine reasons why doing business in Rwanda is a smart strategy. *HOW WE MADE IT IN AFRICA*. Retrieved from http://www.howwemadeitinafrica.com/nine-reasons-why-doing-business-in-rwanda-is-a-smart-strategy/52274/

Boswell, J. (2016, May 13). *Rwanda's gorilla tourism tactics*. [Video file]. Retrieved from http://www.bbc.com/news/business-36284954

Bouie, J. (2014). White people are fine with laws that harm Blacks. *Slate*. Retrieved from http://www.slate. com/articles/health_and_science/science/2014/08/ racial_bias_in_criminal_justice_Whites_don_t_want_to_ reform_laws_that_harm.html

Breasted, J. (1937). A history of Egypt, from the earliest times to the Persian conquest. London, England: Forgotten Books.

British Pathé Series Reporter. (2014, April 13). *Congo harvest – Wealth of the world* (1950). [Video file]. Retrieved from https://www. youtube.com/watch?v=th4Zwv5pvFg

Brown, S. (2011). The dark world of the Arab child slave trade. *FrontPage Mag*. Retrieved from http://www.frontpagemag.com/ fpm/95692/dark-world-arab-child-slave-trade-stephen-brown

Brown, S. (2003). *Fighting for US: Maulana Karenga, the US organization, and Black cultural nationalism.* New York, NY: New York University Press.

Bruns, B., Mingat, A., & Rakotomalala, R. (2003). *A Chance for every child: Achieving universal primary education by 2015.* Washington, DC: The World Bank.

Buzuzi, L. (2016). 10 African myths that really grind my gears. *Huffington Post.* Retrieved from http://www.huffingtonpost. com/entry/10-african-myths-that-really-grind-my-gearslly-grind_us_576d2176e4b06721d4c05e70

Camera, L. (2016). Peer pressure, stereotypes fuel minority students' struggles. *U.S. News & World Report.* Retrieved from http://www.usnews.com/news/articles/2016-05-11/ peer-pressure-stereotypes-fuel-minority-students-struggles

Carney, J., & Rosomoff, R. (2009). *In the shadow of slavery: Africa's botanical legacy in the Atlantic world.* Los Angeles, CA: University of California Press.

Carter, J. (2014). For Black America, the only jobs that await are jobs HBCUs help to create. Huffington Post. Retrieved from http:// www.huffingtonpost.com/jarrett-l-carter/for-Black-america-only-jobs_b_5366657.html

CCTV Africa. (2016, July 3). *Talk Africa: Africa after Brexit.* [Video file]. Retrieved from https://www.youtube.com/ watch?v=4pbSsrv2Nfw

CCTV Africa. (2016, June 11). *Talk Africa: Is a border-less Africa a good or a bad thing?*. [Video file]. Retrieved from https://www.youtube.com/watch?v=CfPhgUul4vo

CCTV America. (2016, July 7). *CCTV News: James Braxton Peterson discusses police involved shootings*. [Video file]. Retrieved from https://www.youtube.com/watch?v=BKtLlrsmdVU

Charig, B. (2012). The Scandinavian nations setting the green energy pace. Blue & Green Tomorrow. Retrieved from http://blueandgreentomorrow.com/features/the-scandinavian-nations-setting-the-green-energy-pace/

Christy, B. (2015). How killing elephants finances terror in Africa. *National Geographic*. Retrieved from http://www.nationalgeographic.com/tracking-ivory/article.html

Christy, B. (2015, September 7). *Ivory's historical connection to the slave trade*. [Video file]. Retrieved from https://www.youtube.com/watch?v=Gitq6_qVCL8

C-Span2. (2016, June 29). *After Words with Heather MacDonald: "The War on Cops: How the New Attack on Law and Order Makes Everyone Less Safe."* [Video file]. Retrieved from http://www.c-span.org/video/?410954-1/words-heather-mac-donald

Clark, C. (2016). Africa's eden: 7 reasons to discover the Waterberg. *CNN*. Retrieved from http://www.cnn.com/2016/05/23/travel/waterberg-south-africa/

CNN. (2012, March 29). *CNN Newsroom: White privilege vs. racial profiling*. [Video file]. Retrieved from https://www.youtube.com/watch?v=EHJN-ozAXK8

Coffle. (n.d.). *Dictionary.com Unabridged.* Retrieved September 24, 2015, from Dictionary.com website: http://dictionary.reference. com/browse/coffle

Cohen, M. (2016). Africa investors look east as commodity-driven boom withers. *Bloomberg.* Retrieved from http://www.bloomberg.com/news/articles/2016-05-12/ africa-investors-look-east-as-commodity-driven-boom-withers

Cohen, M. & Butera, S. (2016). Africa's would-be Switzerland shows economic clout with WEF. *Chicago Tribune.* Retrieved from http://www.chicagotribune.com/news/sns-wp-blm-rwanda-b666b19c-169b-11e6-971a-dadf9ab18869-20160510-story.html

Conniff, R. (1987). When the music in our parlors brought death to darkest Africa. *Audubon.* Retrieved fromhttp://faculty. washington.edu/ellingsn/Conniff-Music-Death-Africa.pdf

Conteh, J. (2013). How African-Americans and African immigrants differ. *the Globalist.* Retrieved from http://www.theglobalist. com/african-americans-african-immigrants-differ/

Craven, J. (2015). Why it isn't possible for Black Americans to appropriate African culture. *Huffington Post.* Retrieved from http://www. huffingtonpost.com/entry/is-it-cultural-appropriation-when-africans-wear-jordans_56099b3be4b0768126fea24d

Cress-Welsing (1991). *Isis papers: The keys to the colors.* Chicago, IL: Third World Press.

Daily Nation Staff Writer.(2014). Israel keen to invest in Kenya, says deputy PM Avigdor Liberman. *Daily Nation.* Retrieved from http://www.nation.co.ke/news/

Israel-keen-to-invest-in-Kenya--says-deputy-PM-Avigdor-Liberman/-/1056/2352912/-/tcbmh3z/-/index.html

Damiba, Pierre-Claver (1988). The challenges of leadership in African development. *Recommendations by Discussion Groups on Economic and Social Issues—Political and Strategic Issues—Inaugural Programme.* Ota, Nigeria: The Africa Leadership Forum. Retrieved from http://www.africaleadership.org/rc/the%20challenges%20of%20leadership%20in%20africa%20development.pdf

Deng, F. M. (1998, August). Report of the discussion group on political and strategic issues. *Recommendations by Discussion Groups on Economic and Social Issues—Political and Strategic Issues—Inaugural Programme.* Ota, Nigeria: The Africa Leadership Forum. Retrieved from http://www.africaleadership.org/rc/the%20challenges%20of%20leadership%20in%20africa%20development.pdf

Dezeen Reporter. (2015). Groosman to create extreme cantilevers for arts centre in Rwanda's capital. *Dezeen.* Retrieved from http://www.dezeen.com/2015/10/07/groosman-kigali-art-culture-centre-rwanda-cantilevered-wings/

Dezeen Reporter. (2015). US firm announces plan to open "the Bauhaus of Africa." *Dezeen.* Retrieved from http://www.dezeen.com/2015/09/24/mass-design-group-african-design-center-architecture-training-school-rwanda-africa/

Douglas, D. (2016). 'Roots' remake strong for kids, but tells brutal truths. *EBONY.* Retrieved from http://www.ebony.com/black-history/roots-reboot-historian#axzz4AEBxZuz2

Dunbar, D. (1991). Everyone wants a piece of Africa now. *Los Angeles Times*. Retrieved from http://articles.latimes.com/1991-10-27/news/vw-1049_1_kente-cloth

Dyson, M. (2016). The color line: Stephen Curry's prominence resurfaces issues of colorism among blacks. *The Undefeated*. Retrieved from https://theundefeated.com/features/light-skinned-vs-dark-skinned/

East Africa Agribusiness Staff Writer. (2014). You can do farming without rain. *East Africa Agribusiness*. Retrieved from http://ea-agribusiness.co.ug/you-can-do-farming-without-rain/

East African Girl. (2012). How beauty can lead to genocide. *East African Girl*. Retrieved from http://eastafricangirl.wordpress.com/2012/12/01/how-beauty-can-lead-to-genocide/

Ebegbulem, J. (2012). Corruption and leadership crisis in Africa: Nigeria in Focus. *International Journal of Business and Social Science, 3*(11), 221-227.

Edwards, Bernard. (2007). *Royal Navy versus the slave traders*. South Yorkshire, England: Pen & Sword Maritime.

Eglash, R. (1999). *African fractals: Modern computing and indigenous design*. Piscataway, NJ: Rutgers University Press.

eNCA. (2014, September 14). *Gabon plans to revive its international centre for Bantu civilizations*. [Video file]. Retrieved from https://www.youtube.com/watch?v=YfgkDow929

Even At The Doors Reporter. (2013, February 16). *Congo war: The most craved after minerals on earth*. [Video file]. Retrieved from https://www.youtube.com/watch?v=Vjn1TLYzMIU

Fallon, A. (2016). Israel is secretly shipping thousands of refuges to Africa. *ThinkProgress*. Retrieved from http://thinkprogress.org/world/2016/07/03/3795250/african-refugees-israel/

Farhat, J. (2012). Israel siphons off Africa's Nile. *Alakhbar-English*. Retrieved from http://english.al-akhbar.com/node/10490

Farrant, L. (1975). *TIPPU TIP and the East African slave trade*. New York, NY: St. Martin's Press, Inc.

Felter, C. (2015). Why does Africa have so many languages?. Retrieved from http://www.csmonitor.com/Science/Science-Notebook/2015/0421/Why-does-Africa-have-so-many-languages

Fihlani, P. (2013). Africa: Where Black is not really beautiful. *BBC News*. Retrieved from http://www.bbc.co.uk/news/world-africa-20444798

Filindra, A. (2016). How racial prejudice helps drive opposition to gun control. *The Washington Post*. Retrieved from https://www.washingtonpost.com/news/monkey-cage/wp/2016/06/21/heres-the-surprising-reason-some-white-americans-oppose-gun-regulation/

Findlay, S. (2015). Culture war brews over S. African golden rhino figure. *AFP*. Retrieved from http://news.yahoo.com/culture-war-brews-over-african-golden-rhino-figurine-044913790.html

Fisher, M. (2013). A revealing map of the world's most and least ethnically diverse countries. *The Washington Post*. Retrieved from https://www.washingtonpost.com/news/worldviews/wp/2013/05/16/a-revealing-map-of-the-worlds-most-and-least-ethnically-diverse-countries/

Foote, M. (2014). African heads summit in US: Black Americans must be proactive. *African Executive.* Retrieved from http://www.africanexecutive.com/modules/magazine/articles.php?article=7901&magazine=502

Foster, M. & Killick, T. (2006). What would doubling aid do for macroeconomic management in Africa?: A synthesis paper. *ODI Working Paper No. 264,* April.

Fulwood, III, S. (2016). America's moved on – but many still live in a white fantasy land. *Newsweek. Retrieved* from http://www.newsweek.com/america-moved-many-still-live-white-fantasy-461223

Furious. (2013). Ghana apologizes to slaves' descendants. *Urban Intellectuals.* Retrieved from http://urbanintellectuals.com/2013/04/15/ghana-apologizes-to-slaves-descendants/

Fu Kiau, K. K. (2001). *African cosmology of the Bantu-Kongo: Tying the spiritual knot, principles of life & living.* New York, NY: Athelia Henrietta Press.

Frangoul, A. (2015). Pay-as-you-go solar power takes off in Africa. *CNBC.* Retrieved from http://www.cnbc.com/2015/02/25/pay-as-you-go-solar-power-takes-off-in-africa.html

French, H. (2014). *China's second continent: How a million migrants are building a new empire in Africa.* New York, NY: Alfred A. Knopf.

Frugé, A. (2016). The opposite of Brexit: African Union launches an all-Africa passport. *The Washington Post.* Retrieved from https://www.washingtonpost.com/news/monkey-cage/wp/2016/07/01/the-opposite-of-brexit-african-union-launches-an-all-africa-passport/

Garrett, G. (1997). Relocating Burton: Public and private writings on Africa. *The Journal of African Travel-Writing*, 2. Retrieved from http://www.unc.edu/~ottotwo/burton.html

Gateway Africa Writer. (n.d.). The Bushman / San of Namibia: The first people of Africa. *Gateway Africa*. Retrieved from http://www.gateway- africa.com/countries/namibia/bushmen.htm

Gates, Jr., H. & Amos, J. (2013). My slave ancestors: From Angola?. *The Root*. Retrieved from http://www.theroot.com/articles/world/2013/06/where_did_slaves_come_from_in_africa_angola_is_one_place.html

Gates, Jr., H. & Pironti, E. (2013). From which port was slave ancestor sold?. *The Root*. Retrieved from http://www.theroot.com/articles/culture/2013/11/from_which_ports_did_angolan_slaves_come.2.html

Gelb, A., Knight, J. & Sabot, R. (1991). Public sector employment, rent seeking, and economic growth. *Economic Journal*, 101 (Sept.), pp. 1186-1199.

Gelman, A. (2016). Why is Africa so poor while Europe and North America are so Wealthy?. *The Washington Post*. Retrieved from https://www.washingtonpost.com/news/monkey-cage/wp/2016/04/24/why-is-africa-so-poor-while-europe-and-north-america-are-so-wealthy/

Giberson, K. (2015). The Biblical roots of racism. *Huffington Post*. Retrieved from http://www.huffingtonpost.com/karl-giberson-phd/the-biblical-roots-of-racism_b_7649390.html

Gluckman, M. (1961). Anthropological problems arising from the African industrial revolution. In A. W. Southall (ed.), *Social Change in Modern Africa*. London, England: OUP.

Goad, J. (2012). Islam's role in slavery. *Taki's Magazine*. Retrieved from http://takimag.com/article/islams_role_in_slavery_jim_goad/print#axzz4CMMhAVAx

Goldenberg, T. & Daraghmeh, M. (2016). Israel's Netanyahu seeks new allies in historic Africa trip. *Associated Press*. Retrieved from https://www.yahoo.com/finance/news/israels-netanyahu-seeks-allies-historic-africa-trip-070050280.html

Grammaticas, D. (2012). Chinese colonialism?. *BBC News*. Retrieved from http://www.bbc.co.uk/news/world-asia-18901656

Grider, G. (2016). Bacha Bazi reveals the dark secret life of Islam's pedophile and homosexual culture. *Now The End Begins*. Retrieved from http://www.nowtheendbegins.com/bacha-bazi-dark-secret-life-of-islams-pedophiles-homosexuals/

Grifalconi, A. (1986). *The village of round and square houses*. New York, NY: Little, Brown and Company.

Grifalconi, A. & Nelson, K. (2002). *The village that vanished*. New York, NY: Dialed Books for Young Readers.

Grinberg, E. (2016). U.S. flags removed from Confederate graves on Memorial Day weekend. *CNN*. Retrieved from http://www.cnn.com/2016/06/07/us/shiloh-national-park-confederate-graves/index.html

Gross, K. (2016). Kali Nicole Gross: Snoop Dogg is wrong about 'Roots,' but right about tv. *The Dallas Morning News*. Retrieved from http://www.dallasnews.com/opinion/latest-columns/20160602-kali-nicole-gross-snoop-dogg-is-wrong-about-roots-but-right-about-tv.ece

Guardian Staff Writer. (2014). South Sudan: Mining act passed, but nation too must benefit. *Guardian*. Retrieved from http://www.theguardian.com/global-development-professionals-network/adam-smith-international-partner-zone/south-sudan-mining-act-adam-smith-international

Hallet, J. (1973). *Pygmy Kitabu: A revealing account of the origin and legends of the African Pygmies*. New York, NY: Random House.

Halliday, J. (2016). Ten reasons why repatriation of blacks us a good idea. *Vanguard News Network*. Retrieved from http://www.vanguardnewsnetwork.com/v1/index409.htm

Hanauer, L., & Morris, L. (2014). In Africa: U.S. promotes security, China does business. African Globe. Retrieved from http://www.africanglobe.net/business/africa-promotes-security-china-business/

Handley, G., Higgins, K., Sharma, B., Bird, K., & Cammack, D. (2009). *Poverty and poverty reduction in Sub-Saharan Africa: An overview of key issues*. London, England: Overseas Development Institute.

Harmon, K. (2011). Middle Eastern Stone Age tools mark earlier date for human migration out of Africa. *Scientific American*. Retrieved from http://www.scientificamerican.com/article/middle-eastern-stone-age-tools/

Harvey, M. (2002). *Look what came from Africa.* New York, NY: Franklin Watts, Inc.

Harvin, M. (2016). Higher status jobs but lower pay for African-Americans graduating from HBCUs. *GoodCall.* Retrieved from https://www.goodcall.com/news/higher-status-jobs-but-lower-pay-for-african-americans-graduating-from-hbcus-03941

Hatzfeld, Jean. (2007). *The Antelope's Strategy: Living in Rwanda after the genocide.* New York, NY: Farrar, Straus, and Giroux.

Hegel, G. (1956).*Philosophy of History.* New York, NY: Dover Publications.

Heine, B. & Nurse, D. (2000). *African Languages: An Introduction.* Cambridge, England: Cambridge University Press.

Herrington, O. A language of their own: Swahili and its influences. *Harvard Political Review.* Retrieved from http://harvardpolitics.com/books-arts/swahili-language-influence/

Heywood, L. & Heywood, J. (2007). *Central Africans, Atlantic Creoles, and the foundation of the Americas, 1585-1660.* New York, NY: Cambridge University Press.

Hill, L. (2016). African countries splashing $30 billion on 11,000kms of railway – it's just what continental trade needs. *Mail & Guardian Africa.* Retrieved from http://mgafrica.com/article/2016-04-08-african-countries-splashing-30-billion-on-11000kms-of-railway-its-just-what-continental-trade-needs

Hilliard, A. (1998). *African power: Affirming African indigenous socialization in the face of the culture wars.* Atlanta, GA: Makare Press.

Hinckley, S. (2015). More Asian than Hispanic immigrants: political implications?. *Christian Science Monitor.* Retrieved from http://news.yahoo.com/more-asian-hispanic-immigrants-political-implications-152954025.html

Hinde, S. (1897). *The fall of the Congo Arabs.* London, England: Methuen & Company.

Holland, J. (2016). Presidential race shows deep seated strife toward minorities. *Associated Press.* Retrieved from https://www.yahoo.com/news/presidential-race-shows-deep-seated-064520592.html

Holloway, J. (Ed.). (1990). *Africanisms in American culture.* Bloomington, IN: Indiana University Press.

Holter, M. (2013). Norway approves $3 billion for wind power plants to triple capacity. RenewableEnergyWorld.com. Retrieved from http://www.renewableenergyworld.com/rea/news/print/article/2013/08/norway-approves-3-billion-for-wind-power-plants-to-triple-capacity

Hood, R. (1994). *Begrimed and Black: Christian traditions on Blacks and Blackness.* Minneapolis, MN: Augsburg Fortress Press.

Howe, S. (1998). *Afrocentrism: Mythical pasts and imagined homes.* London, England: Verso.

Hughes, D. (1994). *Afrocentric architecture: A design primer.* Dayton, OH: Greyden Press.

Ibekwe, P. (1998). *Wit & wisdom of Africa: Proverbs from Africa & the Caribbean.* Trenton, NJ: Africa World Press, Inc.

Imhotep, A. (2009). *The Bakala of North America: In search of a meaningful name for African-Americans*. Charleston, SC: MOCHA-Versity Press.

Indiana University African Studies Website Team. (2014). KiSwahili. *Indiana University African Studies Program*. Retrieved from http://www.indiana.edu/~afrist/academics/languages_kiswahili.shtml

In2EastAfrica. (2013). The East African Community: What we can learn from each other. *TradeMark East Africa*. Retrieved from http://www.trademarkea.com/the-east-african-community-what-we-can-learn-from-each-other/

Invest in Norway Staff Writer. (2014). Energy and environment. *Invest in Norway*. Retrieved from http://www.invinor.no/no/Industries/Energy--Environment/

Jabbar, S. (2014). Who taught you to hate your [dark] skin?. *This Is Africa*. Retrieved from http://thisisafrica.me/who-taught-you-to-hate-your-dark-skin/

Jackson, D. & Jackson, N. (1992). *Escape from the Slave Traders: David Livingstone*. Bloomington, MN: Bethany House Publishers.

Jaschik, S. (2013). Meritocracy or Bias?. *INSIDE HIGHER ED*. Retrieved from https://www.insidehighered.com/news/2013/08/13/white-definitions-merit-and-admissions-change-when-they-think-about-asian-americans

Journal of Experimental Psychology Staff Writer. (2015). Racial anxiety may alter time perceptions for some white Americans, study says. *MedicalXpress*. Retrieved from http://medicalxpress.

com/news/2015-11-racial-anxiety-perception-white-americans.
html

Kabaila, M. (2016). Zambia: Understanding dual citizenship. *AllAfrica*.
Retrieved from http://allafrica.com/stories/201601140399.html

Kaberuka, D. (2012). Economic integration: Time to raise the bar. *The African Executive*. Retrieved fromhttp://www.africanexecutive.
com/modules/magazine/articles.php?article=6828

Kabiza Wilderness Safaris Staff Writer. (2015). Imigongo paintings –
WherecowdungbecomesartinRwanda.*KabizaWildernessSafaris*.
Retrieved from http://kabiza.com/kabiza-wilderness-safaris/
imigongo-paintings-where-cow-dung-becomes-art-in-rwanda/

Kalinaki, D. (2016, July 4). *Benjamin Netanyahu talks about Israel's new engagement with Africa*. [Video file]. Retrieved from https://
www.youtube.com/watch?v=fuR0Ibv6zzo

Karenga, M. (1980). *Kawaida theory: An introductory outline.*
Inglewood, CA: Kawaida Productions.

Karenga, M. (1984). *Selections from the Husia: Sacred wisdom of ancient Egypt*. Los Angeles, CA: The University of Sankore Press.

Kastel, Z. (2011). Noah's curse of Ham, slavery, anti-Black racism & understanding Midrash. *Social Issues and Torah*. Retrieved from
http://torahforsociallyawarehasid.blogspot.com/2011/10/noahs-
curse-of-ham-slavery-anti-black.html

Katembo, B. (2012). *Scattered assets: How African-Americans & other resources can shape 21st century pan-African empowerment*.
Bloomington, IN: AuthorHouse.

Katembo, I. (2002). *Elephants in a bamboo cage: The Black condition, the American psyche, and the next step forward.* Raleigh, NC: Mkuyu Books.

Kaula, E. (1968). *The Bantu Africans.* New York, NY: Franklin Watts, Inc.

Kavuma, R. (2011). Uganda's first electric car proves the potential of Africa's universities. *The Guardian.* Retrieved from http://www. theguardian.com/global-development/poverty-matters /2011/ nov/10/uganda-electric-car-education

Kazeem, Y. (2016). The only way to save African rhinos: ship them to Australia. *Quartz Africa.* Retrieved from http://qz.com/669330/ the-only-way-to-save-african-rhinos-ship-them-to-australia/

Keane, F. (1995). *Season of blood: A Rwandan journey.* London, England: Penguin Books.

Kelto, A. (2015). John Oliver says U.S. students learn virtually nothing about Africa. *NPR.* Retrieved from http://www.npr.org/ sections/goatsandsoda/2015/09/09/438672718/john-oliver-says-u-s-students-learn-virtually-nothing-about-africa?sc=tw

Kenny, A. (2014).Why don't we use the term "Bantu"?. *Politicsweb.* Retrieved from http://politicsweb.co.za/politicsweb/view/ politicsweb/en/page71619?oid=547665&sn=Detail&pid=71619

Khadka, N. (2016). East Asian networks 'smuggle ivory across Africa'. *CNN.* Retrieved from http://www.bbc.com/news/ world-africa-36717989

Kumah-Abiwu, F. (2016). Beyond intellectual construct to policy ideas: The case of the Afrocentric paradigm. *Journal of Pan African*

Studies, 9 (1). [Online]. Retrieved from http://www.jpanafrican. org/docs/vol9no1/9.1-11-Felix.pdf

Kushner, J. (2016). Friday on VICE on HBO: Leaving China in pursuit of the African dream. *VICE NEWS*. Retrieved from https://news. vice.com/article/friday-on-vice-on-hbo-leaving-china-in-pursuit-of-the-african-dream

Kuugongelwa-Amadhila, S. (2015). Branding Namibia. *The African Executive*. Retrieved from http://www.africanexecutive.com/ modules/magazine/articles.php?article=8675&magazine=578

Ladson-Billings, G. (2001). *Dreamkeepers: Successful teachers of African American children*. San Francisco, CA: Jossey-Bass

Lal, D., & Myint, H. (1996). *The political economy of poverty, equity and growth: A comparative study*. Oxford, UK: Clarendon Press.

Land, S. (2016). Chewbacca mom is raking in the cash, but what about people who need it?. *sheknows*. Retrieved from http:// www.sheknows.com/living/articles/1123479/chewbacca-mom

Lavine, S. (1986). *Wonders of giraffes*. New York, NY: Putnam Pub Group Library.

Lefkowitz, M. (1997). *Not out of Africa*. New York, NY: Basic Books.

Leroi, A. (1997). Why rhino-mounted Bantu never sacked Rome. [Review of Guns, Germs, and Steel by J. Diamond.]. *London Review of Books*. Retrieved from http://www.armandmarieleroi. com/?p=360

Levi, J. (Lecturer). (2010). *The history of the Bible and Qu'ran (Part 2): The Arabs: their world, the Qu'ran and their view of African people* [DVD Lecture]. (Available from AfricanHistoryNetwork.com).

Lester, J. (1994). *The man who knew too much: A moral tale from the Baila of Zambia*. New York, New York: Clarion Books.

Ligtvoet, F. (2015). On colonial fairs and 'de-colonizing' American history in elementary school. *Huffington Post*. Retrieved from http://www.huffingtonpost.com/frank-ligtvoet/on-colonial-fairs-and-dec_b_8147054.html

Mafeje, A. (1971). The ideology of tribalism. *The Journal of Modern African Studies, 9*(2): 253–261.

Magee, C. (2011). *Africa in the American imagination: Popular culture, racialized identities and African visual culture*. Jackson, MS: University Press of Mississippi.

Marshall, B. (2015, October 31). *TALK AFRICA: Chinese technology in Africa*. [Video file]. Retrieved from https://www.youtube.com/watch?v=hAsGTNZqGWo

Marsh, J. (2016). The African migrants giving up on the Chinese dream. *CNN*. Retrieved from http://www.cnn.com/2016/06/26/asia/africans-leaving-guangzhou-china/index.html

Mbiti, J. (1992). *African religion and philosophy*. Portsmouth, NH: Heinemann.

M'bokolo, E. (1998). The impact of the slave trade on Africa. *Le Monde diplomatique*. Retrieved from https://mondediplo.com/1998/04/02africa

Mbolela, N. (2016). Zambia: economic benefits of dual citizenship. *Tumfweko*. Retrieved from https://tumfweko.com/2016/01/07/zambia-economic-benefits-of-dual-citizenship/

McLean, M. (n.d.). Slavery – Africa, Europe, and Jamaica. The Dread Library. Retrieved from https://debate.uvm.edu/dreadlibrary/mclean.html

McWhorter, J. (2016). 'Roots' of a new conversation about race. *CNN*. Retrieved from http://www.cnn.com/2016/06/01/opinions/what-coming-to-terms-means-roots-john-mcwhorter/

Medard, J. (1982). The underdeveloped state of Africa: Political clientelisms or neo- patrimonialism. In *Private patronage and public power* (Christopher Clapham, ed.). London, England: Pinter.

Melton, J. V. (1988). *Absolutism and the eighteenth-century origins of compulsory schooling in Prussia and Austria.* New York, NY: Cambridge University Press.

Meredith, M. (2001). *Elephant destiny: Biography of an endangered species of Africa.* New York, NY: Public Affairs.

Mind of Malaka Blogger. (2014). Repatriation: Is going back to Africa the solution?. *Mind of Malaka*. Retrieved from https://mindofmalaka.com/2014/12/04/repatriation-is-going-back-to-africa-the-solution/

Mngodo, E. (2015). Finally! Recognition for Kiswahili writers. *The Citizen*. Retrieved from http://www.thecitizen.co.tz/magazine/success/Finally--Recognition--for-Kiswahili-writers----/-/1843788/2611710/-/io68flz/-/index.html

Mobley, C. (2008). Slave ship's sad saga left no imprint on Savannah. *Savannah Now.* Retrieved from http://savannahnow.com/chuck-mobley/2008-02-29/slave-ships-sad-saga-left-no-imprint-savannah

Mohamed, H. (2015). Zimbabwe's white farmers start anew in Mozambique. *Aljazeera.* Retrieved from http://www.aljazeera.com/indepth/features/2015/10/zimbabwe-white-farmers-start-anew-mozambique-151027095006428.html

Monks, K. (2016). Why the wealth of Africa does not make Africans wealthy. *CNN.* Retrieved from http://www.cnn.com/2016/04/18/africa/looting-machine-tom-burgis-africa/index.html

Moore, A. (2014). 10 facts about the Arab enslavement of black people not taught in schools. *Atlanta Blackstar.* Retrieved from http://atlantablackstar.com/2014/06/02/10-facts-about-the-arab-enslavement-of-black-people-not-taught-in-schools/2/

Moore, J. (2009). From noses to hips, Rwandans start to redefine beauty. *The Christian Science Monitor.* Retrieved from http://www.csmonitor.com/World/Africa/2008/0718/p01s05-woaf.html/(page)/1

Moraga, V. (2011). *Weaving abstraction: Kuba textiles and the woven art of Central Africa.* Washington, DC: The Textile Museum.

Mosupyoe, B., & Ramose, M. (2007). *The development of thought in pan Africanism.* Dubuque, IA: Kendall/Hunt Publishing Company.

Msasanuri, S. (2009). Tanzanian women dying for White skin. *ThisDay.* Retrieved from http://www.thisday.co.tz/?l=10501

Muhammad, S. (2014). Yes African-Americans can claim Africa too. *Huffington Post*. Retrieved from http://www.huffingtonpost. com/shamira-muhammad/time-does-not-exist_b_8103906. html

Musewe, V. (2014). The Black man's burden. *The African Executive*. Retrieved from http://www.africanexecutive.com/modules/ magazine/articles.php?article=7645

Mwagiru, Ciugu. Kiswahili has spread beyond region, thrives in unexpected places. *Pan African Visions*. Retrieved from http:// panafricanvisions.com/2012/kiswahili-has-spread-beyond-region-thrives-in-unexpected-places/

Mwewa, C. (2015). 10 reasons why dual citizenship is good for Zambia. *The African Executive*. Retrieved from http:// www.africanexecutive.com/modules/magazine/articles. php?article=7645

Mwongeli, S. (2015, April 9). *The Black Barbie: A South African doll kids can identify with*. [Video file]. Retrieved from https://www. youtube.com/watch?v=_IoUjOhhSeE

Naqvi, M. (2016). Africans in India face constant battles with racism. *The Roanoke Times*. Retrieved from http://www.roanoke. com/africans-in-india-face-constant-battles-with-racism/ article_59a502d7-fc26-5ae6-8369-3bfcd81283f1.html

Ndaba, O. (2012). Why China will not solve Africa's problems. *The African Executive*. Retrieved from http://www.africanexecutive. com/modules/magazine/articles.php?article=6753

Negrero. (n.d.). Wiktionary. Retrieved May 09, 2015, from http://en.wiktionary.org/wiki/negrero

Negro. (n.d.). *Online Etymology Dictionary.* Retrieved May 09, 2015, from http://dictionary.reference.com/browse/negro

Neighbor. (n.d.). *Dictionary.com Unabridged.* Retrieved October 23, 2015, from Dictionary.com website: http://dictionary.reference.com/browse/neighbor?s=t

Nelson, B. & Lundin, S. (2010). *Ubuntu!: An inspiring story about an African tradition of teamwork and collaboration.* New York, NY: Crown Publishing Group.

Newscast Media Staff Writer. (2014). Israel and South Sudan sign treaty over rights of River Nile.Newscast Media. Retrieved from http://newscastmedia.com/blog/2012/07/30/israel-and-south-sudan-sign-treaty-over-rights-of-river-nile/

Ngambi, M. and Katembo, B. (2006). HBCUs: A think tank resource for Africa. *Journal of Pan African Studies,* 1 (6). [Online]. Retrieved from http://www.jpanafrican.org/docs/vol1no6/HistoricallyBlackCollegesandUniversities_vol1no6.pdf

Ngatia, A. (2012). Why Africa lags behind. *The African Executive.* Retrieved from http://www.africanexecutive.com/modules/magazine/articles.php?article=6818

Niger. (n.d.). Latin Dictionary. Retrieved May 09, 2015, from http://latindictionary.wikidot.com/adjective: niger

Nkosi, M. (2016, May 13). *Can technology help revolutionise Rwanda's economy?.* [Video file]. Retrieved from http://www.bbc.com/news/business-36284952

Noonan, Jr., J. T. (1977). *The Antelope: The ordeal of the recaptured Africans in the administrations of James Monroe and John Quincy Adams*. Los Angeles, CA: University of California Press.

Norman, A. (2015). Why White parents won't choose Black schools. *Huffington Post*. Retrieved from http://www.huffingtonpost. com/abby-norman2/why-white-parents-wont-ch_b_8294908. html

Nurse, E. (2016). Ethiopian bamboo: the new green gold of Africa?. *CNN*. Retrieved from www.cn.com/2016/04/07/africa/ethiopia-bamboo-mpa/index.html

Nwulia, M. (1975). *Britain and slavery in east Africa*. Washington, DC: Three Continents Press.

Nyang, R. (2015, October 2). *Fastjet's gm explains reasons for basing in Tanzania*. [Video file]. Retrieved from https://www. youtube.com/watch?v=2m2hUmMW4l4&ebc=ANyPxKpY k2PJ6l4LlMtM-uyWcsDyepZ_PZwdLRXpizWNkYyeUZslsW aQBad19UIkphAi8iY_MpWCJt69cck_nicSyu4Nam9xFA

Ochieng, P. (2016). Borrowing is what enriches our languages. *Daily Nation*. Retrieved from http://www.nation.co.ke/oped/Opinion/ Borrowing-is-what-enriches-our-languages/-/440808/3018272/- /13xhy5v/-/index.html

Ochieng, P. (2016). The origin and meaning of the word 'Bantu.' *Daily Nation*. Retrieved from http://www.nation.co.ke/ oped/Opinion/The-origin-and-meaning-of-the-word-Bantu/- /440808/2726486/-/11p2qxe/-/index.html

Ochieng, P. (2016). What the human tribe needs to chop off is only the 'foreskin of the mind.' *Daily Nation*. Retrieved from http://www.nation.co.ke/oped/Opinion/What-the-human-tribe-needs-to-chop-off/-/440808/2593068/-/krhidv/-/index.html

Oguntoyinbo, L. (2014). HBCUs looking abroad in effort to remain competitive. *Diverse*. Retrieved from http://diverseeducation.com/article/66454/

Olander, E. & van Staden, C. (2016). Nigerian in China: Why people here are so racist against black people?. *The Huffington Post*. Retrieved from http://www.huffingtonpost.com/entry/china-racist-black-people_us_576a9840e4b065534f485002

Omondi, C. (2011). S. Sudan is the next Kiswahili frontier. *H-Net Online*. Retrieved from http://h-net.msu.edu/cgi-bin/logbrowse.pl?trx=vx&list=H-Swahili&month=1101&week=b&msg=h3bOP81Y3vjSU9meU4jeUw

Omoniyi, T. (2012). Nigeria: Gembu—An untapped nature's gift. *AllAfrica*. Retrieved from http://allafrica.com/stories/201207230398.html

Onyango-Obbo, C. (2016). Xenophobia in Zambia: Why it won't happen in east Africa. *NTV*. Retrieved from http://ntv.co.ug/blogs/charles-onyango-obbo/2016/apr/25/xenophobia-zambia-why-it-won%E2%80%99t-happen-east-africa#sthash.PLnABa6h.dpbs

Opobo, M. (2013). Rwanda hosts first-ever EAC arts and culture fest. *The New Times*. Retrieved from http://www.newtimes.co.rw/news/index.php?i=15263&a=63739

Osborne, H. (2015). Warlords of ivory: Investigation looks at elephant poaching business with fake tusks and a GPS device. *International Business Times*. Retrieved from http://www.ibtimes.co.uk/warlords-ivory-investigation-looks-elephant-poaching-business-fake-tusks-gps-device-1517660

O'Reilly, B. (2016). Bill O'Reilly: How Black Lives Matter is killing Americans. *Fox News*. Retrieved from http://www.foxnews.com/transcript/2016/05/26/bill-oreilly-how-black-lives-matter-is-killing-americans/?hl=1&noRedirect=1

Owen, D. (1985). *None of the above: The truth behind the SATs*. Lanham, MD: Rowan & Littlefield

Paglia, P. (2014). African conflicts and the role of ethnicity: A case study of Sudan. Retrieved from http://www.africaeconomicanalysis.org/articles/pdf/sudan0807.pdf

Pailey, R. (2016). Where is the 'African' in African studies?. *African Arguments*. Retrieved from http://africanarguments.org/2016/06/07/where-is-the-african-in-african-studies/

Palet, L. (2016). The new safari: Kiss colonialism (and khakis) goodbye. *OZY*. Retrieved from http://www.ozy.com/fast-forward/the-new-safari-kiss-colonialism-and-khakis-goodbye/67619

Pilling, D. (2015). Africa ties with China are about more than raw materials. *The New Africa*. Retrieved from http://www.ft.com/intl/cms/s/0/e6b692ec-5e2f-11e5-a28b-50226830d644.html#axzz3nkncYnEl

Pitner, B. (2015). African Americans can't go 'home'. *The Daily Beast*. Retrieved from http://www.thedailybeast.com/articles/2015/10/21/african-americans-can-t-go-home.html

Prussin, L. (1974, October). An Introduction to Indigenous African Architecture. *Journal of the Society of Architectural Historian, 33*(3), 182-205.

Reed, J. (2016). Israel looks to Africa for new allies. Financial Times. Retrieved from https://next.ft.com/content/2c4123a8-ef59-11e5-9f20-c3a047354386

Reuters Staff Writer. (2010). Israel to share agricultural know-how with struggling African farmers.*Haaretz*. Retrieved from http://www.haaretz.com/news/diplomacy-defense/israel-to-share-agricultural-know-how-with-struggling-african-farmers-1.284919

Reynolds, J. (2007). China in Africa: Developing ties. *BBC News*. Retrieved from http://news.bbc.co.uk/2/hi/6264476.stm

Rincon, P. (2003). Tanzania, Ethiopia origin of humans. *BBC News*. Retrieved from http://news.bbc.co.uk/2/hi/science/nature/2909803.stm

Roithmayr, D. (2014). *Reproducing Racism: How everyday choices lock in White advantage*. New York, NY: New York University Press.

Rosenberg, M. (2016). African politics can help us understand why so many white people support Donald Trump. *QUARTZ*. Retrieved from http://qz.com/699419/african-politics-can-help-us-understand-why-so-many-white-people-support-donald-trump/

Rucker, A. (2011). Sudan's wildlife migration miracle. *Frontlines*. Retrieved from http://www.usaid.gov/news-information/frontlines/sudan-south-sudaneducation/sudan%E2%80%99s-wildlife-migration-miracle

Rushing, E. (2013). David Livingstone and the other slave trade, part I. *Smithsonian Libraries*. Retrieved from https://blog.library.si.edu/2013/09/david-livingstone-and-the-other-slave-trade-part-i/

Rushing, E. (2013). David Livingstone and the other slave trade, part II. *Smithsonian Libraries*. Retrieved from http://blog.library.si.edu/2013/10/david-livingstone-and-the-other-slave-trade-part-ii-the-arab-slave-trade/

Rushing, E. (2013). David Livingstone and the other slave trade, part III. *Smithsonian Libraries*. Retrieved from http://blog.library.si.edu/2013/10/david-livingstone-and-the-other-slave-trade-part-iii-the-slaver-and-the-abolitionist/

Saidykhan, S. (2010). Founding a new African "tribe." *Sahara Reporters*. Retrieved from http://saharareporters.com/article/founding-new-african-%E2%80%9Ctribe%E2%80%9D

Saka, H. (2012). Internal conflict: Africa's undoing. *The African Executive*. Retrieved from http://www.africanexecutive.com/modules/magazine/articles.php?article=6958

Sales, B. (2014). With Israeli tech, Amiran Kenya looks to boost East Africa's farmers. *JTA*. Retrieved from http://www.jta.org/2014/02/18/news-opinion/world/with-israeli-tech-amiran-kenya-looks-to-boost-east-africas-farmers

Schuster, J. (1999). Israelis harness sun, saline water to transform desert. *Jweekly.com*. Retrieved from http://www.jweekly.com/article/full/9981/israelis-harness-sun-saline-water-to-transform-desert/

Sebuhayi, J. & Ntigulirwa, A. (2016, March 3). *MASS architects: Africa's architects must understand their continent.* [Video file]. Retrieved from https://www.youtube.com/watch?v=dPnULrKS_rQ

Shapshak, T. (2015, October 23). *"Pay-as-you-go" energy for off-grid customers.* [Video file]. Retrieved from https://www.youtube.com/watch?v=kmwCk8pgWsU

Shah, N. (2016). Our reaction to Harambe the gorilla – and the black boy who fell into his cage – has everything to do with race. *Independent*. Retrieved from http://www.independent.co.uk/voices/our-reaction-to-the-death-of-harambe-the-gorilla-and-the-black-toddler-who-was-saved-has-everything-a7059796.html

Shahadah, O. (2014). Cultural footprints: How does Africa fare? *The African Executive*. Retrieved from http://www.africanexecutive.com/modules/magazine/articles.php?article=7676

Shikwati, J. (2009). Africa must probe the invented wheel. *The African Executive*. Retrieved from http://www.africanexecutive.com/modules/magazine/article_print.php?article=4801

Shockley, K. (2007). Literatures and definitions: Toward understanding Africentric education. *Journal of Negro Education, 76*(2).

Shockley, K., Bond, H., & Rollins, J. (2008). Singing in my own voice: Teachers' journey toward self-knowledge. *Journal of Transformative Education, 6*(3).

Shockley, K., & Frederick, R. (2010). Constructs and dimensions of Afrocentric education. *Journal of Black Studies, 40*(6).

Siddle, J. (2013). What if Africa were to become the hub for global science?. *BBC.* Retrieved from http://www.bbc.com/news/science-environment-21851042

Silver, M. (2016). Only April fools think Africa is a country!. *NPR.* Retrieved from http://www.npr.org/sections/goatsandsoda/2016/04/01/472692287/only-april-fools-think-africa-is-a-country

Sithole, N. (1969). *African nationalism.* New York, NY: Oxford University Press.

Slaughter, J. (2005). *Brother in the bush: An African American's search for self in east Africa.* Chicago, IL: Agate Publishing.

Smith, D. (2009). African chiefs urged to apologise for slave trade. *The Guardian.* Retrieved from http://www.theguardian.com/world/2009/nov/18/africans-apologise-slave-trade

Smith, D. (2012). China's booming trade with Africa helps tone its diplomatic muscle. *The Guardian.* Retrieved from http://www.theguardian.com/world/2012/mar/22/chinas-booming-trade-africa-diplomatic

Sparks, R. (2014). *Where the Negroes are masters: An African port in the era of the slave trade.* Cambridge, MA: Harvard University Press.

Spicer, J., Davis, N. Z., Lowe, L., & Vision, B. (2012). *Revealing the African presence in renaissance Europe.* Baltimore, MD: Walters Art Museum.

Srivastava, V., & Larizza, M. (2012). *Working with the grain for reforming the public service: A live example from Sierra Leone.* Washington, DC: World Bank.

Sterbenz, C., & Bender, J. (2015). National Geographic put a GPS tracker device inside a fake ivory tusk - here's where it went. *Business Insider.* Retrieved from http://www.businessinsider. com/this-detailed-map-shows-how-terrorists-use-elephant-ivory-to-fund-violence-2015-9

Stern, S. (2007). It's time to face the whole truth about the Atlantic slave trade. *History News Network.* Retrieved from http:// historynews network.org/article/41431

Stuart-Mogg, D. (2010). *Mlozi of Central Africa, trader, slaver and self-styled sultan: The end of the slaver.* Blantyre, Malawi: Central Africana Limited.

Sutton, J. (1968). *The east African coast.* [Published as paper no. 1 for the Historical Association of Tanzania]. Nairobi, Kenya: East African Publishing House.

Swahili Language. (n.d.) Maeneo penye wasemaji wa Kiswahili. In *Wikipedia.* Retrieved November 1, 2015 from https:// en.wikipedia.org/wiki/Swahili_language#/media/ File:Maeneo_penye_wasemaji_wa_Kiswahili.png)

Swann, A. (1910). *Fighting the slave-hunters in Central Africa: A record of twenty-six years of travel and adventures round the Great Lakes.* London, England: Seeley, Service and Company, Limited.

Swartz, A. (2016). How Stanford rapist Brock Turner's mugshot express a double standard in the media. *News. Mic.* Retrieved from https://mic.com/articles/145488/

how-stanford-rapist-brock-turner-s-mugshot-exposes-a-double-standard-in-the-media#.4AUwMhhxh

The Advise Show TV. (2015, May 20). *White vs. black open carry social experiment exposes racism with police.* [Video file]. Retrieved from https://www.youtube.com/watch?v=jf5TEoo-EYo

Thiong'o, N. (2009). *Something torn and new: An African renaissance.* New York, NY: BasicCivitas Books.

Thome, W. (2014). South Sudan creates Ministry for Tourism and Wildlife Conservation. *e-TurboNews.* Retrieved from http://www.eturbonews.com/43797/south-sudan-creates-ministry-tourism-and-wildlife-conservation

Times of Zambia Reporter. (2014). Zambia: Of Chitenges and Ankaras. *allAfrica.* Retrieved from http://allafrica.com/stories/201409010829.html

Tsavo Trust. (2012-2014). Giant Tsavo Elephant Bull Tusker [Online image]. *The Tsavo Trust Website.* Retrieved November 7, 2015 from http://tsavotrust.org/support-tsavo-tuskers/

Twitty, M. (2015). Barbeque is an American tradition – of enslaved Africans and Native Americans. *The Guardian.* Retrieved from http://www.theguardian.com/commentisfree/2015/jul/04/barbecue-american-tradition-enslaved-africans-native-americans

United Nations Development Programme (2013). The MDG Report 2013: Assessing Progress in Africa Toward the Millennium Development Goals. Retrieved from http://www.undp.org/

content/undp/en/home/librarypage/mdg/mdg-reports/
africa-collection/

Vass, W. (1979). *The Bantu speaking heritage of the United States*. Los Angeles, CA: UCLA Center for Afro-American Studies.

Wade, N. (2009). Eden? Maybe. But where's the apple tree?. *The New York Times*. Retrieved from http://www.nytimes.com/2009/05/01/science/01eden.html?_r=0

Waller, H. (1874). *The last journals of David Livingstone, in Central Africa, from 1865 to his death, Volume 1 (of 2)*. London, England: Cambridge University Press.

Warner, T. (2016). Racism and stereotypes: how the Tarzan dynamic still infiltrates cinema. *Orlando*. Retrieved from http://weareorlando.co.uk/page13.php

Washington, I. (2011). *A man from another land: How finding my roots changed my life*. New York, NY: Center Street.

Watson, J. (2007). Speech: Nobel Prize Lecture. Retrieved from http://en.wikipedia.org/wiki/James_Watson

Watkins, B. (2016, May 22). *The white woman pic at Huffington Post shows that even liberals don't like black people*. [Video file]. Retrieved from https://www.youtube.com/watch?v=GWsXV_1b4Yw

Weeks, J. (1999). Tarzan and the race card. *The Baltimore Sun*. Retrieved from http://articles.baltimoresun.com/1999-06-27/entertainment/9906280262_1_tarzan-stories-edgar-rice-burroughs-tarzan-means-white-skin

Wekesa, B. (2012). Soft power: Novel ideas for East Africa. *The African Executive.* Retrieved from http://www.africanexecutive.com/modules/magazine/articles.php?article=6909

Whitworth, J. A. G., Kokwaro, G., Kinyanjui, S., Snewin, V.A., Tanner, M., Walport, M., et al. (2008). Strengthening capacity for health research in Africa. *The Lancet, 372*(9649),1590–1593.

Wildlife Conservation Society Staff Writer. (2013). South Sudan expands efforts to protect remaining elephants. *Wildlife Conservation Society.* Retrieved from http://www.wcs.org/press/press-releases/south-sudan-protects-elephants.aspx

Wilson, A. (1993). *Falsification of African consciousness.* Brooklyn, NY: African World InfoSystems.

Wilson, D., & Ayerst, P. (1976). *White gold: The story of African ivory.* New York, NY: Taplinger Publishing Co.

Wright, M. (1993). *Strategies of slaves and women: Life-stories from east/central Africa.* Suffolk, UK: James Currey/Lilian Barber

Womakuyu, F. (2010). Ugandans fight malaria with mosquito eating plants. *New Vision.* Retrieved from http://www.newvision.co.ug/D/8/12/719940

Workneh, K. (2016). It's time to put these myths about the Civil War to rest. *The Huffington Post.* Retrieved from http://www.huffingtonpost.com/entry/4-civil-war-myths_us_576e9934e4b017b379f621e7

Zaslavsky, C. (1999). *Africa counts: Number and pattern in African cultures.* Chicago, IL: Lawrence Hill Books.

Printed in the United States
By Bookmasters